my **revisi⏻n** notes

AQA GCSE
RELIGIOUS STUDIES
RELIGION AND LIFE ISSUES AND RELIGION AND MORALITY

The Publishers would like to thank the following for permission to reproduce copyright material:

Photo credits **P.119** © Lesley Parry

Hachette UK's policy is to use papers that are natural, renewable and recyclable products and made from wood grown in sustainable forests. The logging and manufacturing processes are expected to conform to the environmental regulations of the country of origin.

Orders: please contact Bookpoint Ltd, 130 Milton Park, Abingdon, Oxon OX14 4SB. Telephone: +44 (0)1235 827720. Fax: +44 (0)1235 400454. Lines are open 9.00a.m.–5.00p.m., Monday to Saturday, with a 24-hour message answering service. Visit our website at www.hoddereducation.co.uk

© Lesley Parry, Kim Hands, Jan Hayes 2014
First published in 2014 by
Hodder Education,
An Hachette UK Company
Carmelite House, 50 Victoria Embankment,
London EC4Y 0DZ

Impression number 10 9 8 7 6
Year 2018 2017 2016

Cover photo © Scanrail – Fotolia
Illustrations by Datapage (India) Pvt. Ltd
Typeset in 12/14 Cronospro Light by Datapage (India) Pvt. Ltd.
Printed in India
A catalogue record for this title is available from the British Library
ISBN 978-1-471-80130-3

my revision notes

AQA GCSE
RELIGIOUS STUDIES
RELIGION AND LIFE ISSUES AND RELIGION AND MORALITY

Lesley Parry,
Kim Hands, Jan Hayes

HODDER
EDUCATION
AN HACHETTE UK COMPANY

Contents and revision planner

06   Get the most from this book

Religion and life issues (AQA B unit 2 40552)

	Revised	Tested
Topic 1 Religion and animal rights		
14 Topic basics 1: Humans and animals	☐	☐
15 Topic basics 2: How humans use animals	☐	☐
18 Topic basics 3: Treatment of animals and diet	☐	☐
Topic 2 Religion and planet Earth		
22 Topic basics 1: The origins of life	☐	☐
23 Topic basics 2: The Earth's problems	☐	☐
27 Topic basics 3: Looking after the world	☐	☐
28 Topic basics 4: Religious attitudes to planet Earth	☐	☐
Topic 3 Religion and prejudice		
31 Topic basics 1: What are prejudice and discrimination?	☐	☐
33 Topic basics 2: Attitudes to the key types of prejudice	☐	☐
35 Topic basics 3: Responding to prejudice	☐	☐
36 Topic basics 4: Famous individuals	☐	☐
Topic 4 Religion and early life		
40 Topic basics 1: About children	☐	☐
41 Topic basics 2: Arguments for and against abortion	☐	☐
42 Topic basics 3: Religious attitudes to abortion	☐	☐
43 Topic basics 4: Quality of life and the question of rights	☐	☐
Topic 5 Religion, war and peace		
48 Topic basics 1: Key concepts about war	☐	☐
49 Topic basics 2: Just War and Holy War	☐	☐
51 Topic basics 3: War in the modern world	☐	☐
52 Topic basics 4: Responses to war and peace	☐	☐
Topic 6 Religion and young people		
56 Topic basics 1: Birth ceremonies	☐	☐
58 Topic basics 2: Ceremonies of commitment	☐	☐
60 Topic basics 3: Young people and religion	☐	☐

Religion and morality (AQA B unit 3 40553)

Revised   Tested

Topic 1 Religious attitudes to medical ethics
64   Topic basics 1: Life ☐ ☐
65   Topic basics 2: Fertility treatment ☐ ☐
66   Topic basics 3: Helping medicine ☐ ☐
67   Topic basics 4: Frankenstein sciences ☐ ☐

Topic 2 Religious attitudes to the elderly and death
72   Topic basics 1: The elderly ☐ ☐
73   Topic basics 2: Life after death ☐ ☐
74   Topic basics 3: Caring for the dying ☐ ☐
75   Topic basics 4: Euthanasia ☐ ☐

Topic 3 Religious attitudes to drug abuse
79   Topic basics 1: Mind and body ☐ ☐
80   Topic basics 2: Legal drugs ☐ ☐
82   Topic basics 3: Illegal drugs ☐ ☐
83   Topic basics 4: Drug use and addiction ☐ ☐

Topic 4 Religious attitudes to crime and punishment
87   Topic basics 1: Crime and the causes of crime ☐ ☐
88   Topic basics 2: Aims of punishment ☐ ☐
90   Topic basics 3: Punishments and attitudes to offenders ☐ ☐
92   Topic basics 4: Capital punishment ☐ ☐

Topic 5 Religious attitudes to rich and poor in British society
95   Topic basics 1: Poverty in British society ☐ ☐
96   Topic basics 2: Gambling and the National Lottery ☐ ☐
99   Topic basics 3: Wealth in Britain ☐ ☐
100 Topic basics 4: Helping the poor in Britain ☐ ☐

Topic 6 Religious attitudes to world poverty
104 Topic basics 1: About worldwide poverty ☐ ☐
105 Topic basics 2: Causes of poverty ☐ ☐
107 Topic basics 3: Helping the poor in LEDCs ☐ ☐
110 Topic basics 4: Charitable organisations ☐ ☐

Revision materials

Revised   Tested

113 Revision materials ☐ ☐
119 Revision techniques ☐ ☐
127 Notes ☐ ☐

Get the most from this book

Introduction

REVISION. It's that horrible word we don't like hearing! It is used by teachers a lot but, what do they actually want you to do? Revision is a means to an end. It is a process of learning to enable us to sit an exam and pass it. But how do we do it? Is there a right way or wrong way?

I hate revision

Well, as the writers of this guide, we can assure you we asked the same questions at all levels of our education (and we didn't always enjoy revising either!); we all teach students currently; we are all examiners with lots of experience; and we want you to pass your exams and give yourselves the best options in your future.

The simple fact is revision has to be done if you want to succeed. Much of it will be left for you to do yourselves. Lots of assumptions will be made – that you know what you are doing, that you have a quiet place to work, that your family is supportive of your revision, and that you can handle the pressure to do well. Ideally you will be organised enough to set aside time each day, probably starting three, four or five months prior to the exam. We understand all these assumptions aren't right for everybody, so this guide provides good revision tips to help no matter how you revise.

How are we supposed to learn all this?

This book assumes that you have already studied all the topic material and are now in a position to revise. Our aim is to start to narrow down WHAT you need to know, give you tips on HOW to learn it, think about the TYPE of exam questions you could be asked and, most importantly, give you the CONFIDENCE to know you have prepared well.

How does it work?

- Each topic lists the key terms you need to know so that you can answer questions.

- Each topic is written in bitesize chunks – read and learn it all.

- Next comes some useful teachings – examiners like to read these in your answers as it shows you have studied religious attitudes, which is what the course is all about.

They tell us to revise but I don't know how!

- Then you will get a chance to practise some exam-style questions for the topic – practising makes you very good, as you learn to answer effectively.

- If you are stuck for how to revise, a whole section gives revision techniques to try out – try them all at least once, and don't just try them in RS (they work in any subject).

- Quick tips and hints are scattered throughout the book – quick revision tips, what to do or avoid in your answers, typical mistakes that candidates make in their exam, and checkpoints so you can annotate pages when you are clear on them.

Well guys I think we can answer these issues in a variety of ways

- Additionally, the contents pages allow you to chart your progress on each topic. You should feel your confidence build as you work through those boxes, while at the same time seeing how much more you need to do.

Good luck!

Features to help you succeed

These revision notes will help you to revise for Religion and Life Issues (AQA B unit 2 40552) and Religion and Morality (AQA B unit 3 40553). It is essential to review your work, learn it and test your understanding. Tick each box when you have:

- revised and understood a topic
- checked your understanding and practised the exam questions.

You can also keep track of your revision by ticking off each topic heading in the book. You may find it helpful to add your own notes as you work through each topic.

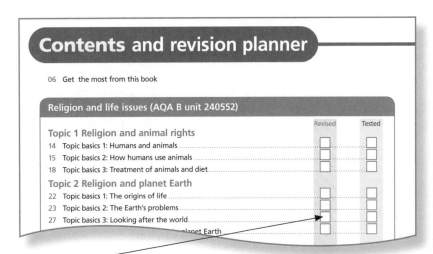

Contents and revision planner

06 Get the most from this book

Religion and life issues (AQA B unit 240552)

	Revised	Tested
Topic 1 Religion and animal rights		
14 Topic basics 1: Humans and animals	☐	☐
15 Topic basics 2: How humans use animals	☐	☐
18 Topic basics 3: Treatment of animals and diet	☐	☐
Topic 2 Religion and planet Earth		
22 Topic basics 1: The origins of life	☐	☐
23 Topic basics 2: The Earth's problems	☐	☐
27 Topic basics 3: Looking after the world	☐	☐

Tick to track your own progress

Exam practice

Practice exam questions provided for each topic. Use them to consolidate your revision and practise your exam skills.

Online

A selection of answers to the exam practice questions in this revision guide are provided on Hodderplus. There is one example given for each mark band as well as helpful advice. Go to www.hodderplus.co.uk.

Religious teachings

Learn some important teachings from each religion for each topic. You can find these teachings throught the book. See page 8 for what they look like.

Exam practice

What questions on this topic look like: Religion and planet Earth
Check back to pages 11–12 to see the grids examiners use to help you mark your answers.

This page contains a range of examples of questions that could be on an exam paper for this topic. Practise them all to strengthen your knowledge and technique while revising. Check the website for answers to some of these, with tips.

1	What is meant by pollution?	[1]
2	What is meant by stewardship?	[1]
3	Explain what is meant by global warming.	[2]
4	Give **two** ways in which humans damage the world.	[2]
5	Explain why some religious believers think it is wrong to destroy the natural environment.	[3]
6	Explain how humans can look after the world.	[3]
7	'Damaging the world is disrespectful to God.' What do you think? Explain your opinion.	[3]
8	Explain religious attitudes to the use of natural resources. Refer to beliefs and teachings in your answer.	[4]
9	Explain **two** ways in which religious people can work for the conservation of the planet.	[4]
10	Explain religious attitudes to the environment. Use religious beliefs and teachings in your answer.	[4]
11	Explain religious attitudes to destruction of the environment. Refer to religious beliefs and teachings in your answer.	[5]
12	Explain the ways in which governments have worked to help the planet.	[5]
13	Describe the ways in which modern living is putting pressure on the environment.	[5]
14	'Humans should respect the world because God created it.' Do you agree? Explain your reasons, showing you have thought about more than one point of view. Refer to religious arguments in your answer.	[6]
15	'Climate change is the biggest problem for humans.' Do you agree? Explain your reasons, showing you have thought about more than one point of view. Refer to religious arguments in your answer.	[6]
16	'Religious people should do the most to look after the planet.' Do you agree? Explain your reasons, showing you have thought about more than one point of view. Refer to religious arguments in your answer.	[6]

Exam tip
Did you know that F-grade candidates usually write very little. They usually only give one idea in any answer. They only know a bit of everything they need to know. If this is you, make sure you double the numbers of points you make in each answer.
Did you know that C-grade candidates write quite a lot, but often do not clearly make their points. They usually don't consistently explain themselves – sometimes they do, sometimes they don't. They know quite a lot about the subject, but not the details. By knowing the information in depth, you can improve this.
Did you know that A-grade candidates write lots. They explain most of the points they make. They use lots of religious words for things. They obviously know their stuff really well.
So, which are you?

Topic 3 Religion and prejudice

Key knowledge
- Different types of prejudice and examples of each.
- Why people are prejudiced, and how they show it.
- Relevance of tolerance, justice, harmony and the value of each person.
- Religious attitudes to prejudice.
- Religious attitudes to:
  o racism
  o sexism
  o homophobia
  o ageism
  o religious prejudice.
- How religions help the victims of prejudice and discrimination.
- What specific individuals have done to fight prejudice.
- What pressure groups and the government have done, e.g. The Race Relation Art.

Topic basics 1: What are prejudice and discrimination?

The exam often asks about what key words mean, such as **prejudice**, **discrimination** and **racism**. It also often asks why people become prejudiced, and how they show it. This topic basic tries to tackle those questions.

Key terms
Discrimination – putting prejudicial thoughts into action
Prejudice – pre-judge someone without evidence (negative thought)
Racism – discrimination on the grounds of colour of skin (race)

Types of prejudice

There are many different types of prejudice, and some are focused on in the exam:
- Racism, e.g. calling someone names because of their colour.
- Sexism, e.g. refusing someone a job because of their gender.
- Ageism, e.g. not listening to someone's opinion because of their age.
- Homophobia, e.g. someone being attacked because the attacker thinks they are gay.
- Religious prejudice, e.g. killing people of a certain faith because of what they believe.

Key terms
Ageism – discrimination on the grounds of being old, middle aged or young (age)
Homophobia – discrimination on the grounds of sexuality (gay or lesbian)
Religious prejudice – discrimination on the grounds of faith or belief
Sexism – discrimination on the grounds of being male or female (gender or sex)

Common mistakes
Candidates mix up 'Why' and 'How' questions so read questions carefully. 'How religious believers fight prejudice' is not the same as 'why' they do.

Exam tip
Learn the definition of each of these and an example of it in action. This will help you answer one-, two-, or three-mark AO1 questions.

Key knowledge
A summary of the things you need to know for each topic.

Common mistakes
Identifies common mistakes that candidates make.

Key term
Clear, concise definitions of essential terms are provided where they appear on the page.

Exam tip
Throughout the book there are tips to help you boost your final grade.

Religious teachings that can be used in all topics

For each religion you study there are several key beliefs and teachings that you can use to support your answers to questions about the attitudes of religions to any topic in the guide. Learn those for the religion(s) you have studied.

Many of these can be applied to a variety of topics so **one** teaching can be used again and again – **less learning**! And across religions – **less learning**!

Exam tip

Choose a teaching and list the topics it could be used in. This makes learning easy because it gives you a set of teachings to learn, and makes you think where they fit.

Buddhism

- Karma – our words and actions shape our future. We need to make sure these are positive.
- Each of the actions of the Eightfold Path – Right Speech, Action, Intention, Awareness, Mindfulness, Livelihood, Effort, Concentration.
- Compassion and metta.
- The Five Precepts:
  - ahimsa
  - not clouding the mind
  - kind language
  - not taking what is not freely given
  - no sexual misconduct.

Sikhism

- Sikh values of sharing, sewa, duty, tolerance, chastity, humility.
- The Khalsa vows:
  - meditation and service to God
  - no use of intoxicants
  - do not eat meat that has been ritually killed
  - equality of all
  - fight injustice
  - not to hurt others.
- All life is sacred, and must be protected and preserved.

Christianity

- Jesus said, Love God, love your neighbour.
- The Ten Commandments.
- God created us all equal as he made us all.
- Justice – everyone is equal so we all deserve fairness.
- Forgiveness, love and compassion.
- Life is sacred.
- God created the world and all in it.

Judaism

- Ten Commandments:
  - Love G-d, do not worship idols, do not misuse G-d's name, keep Shabbat.
  - Respect parents, do not kill, steal, commit adultery, tell lies, do not want what others have.
  - Life is sacred and God-given.
- God created the world and all in it for our use.
- Equality, love, respect.

Islam

- Ummah – brotherhood of all Muslims so all Muslims are equal and deserve respect, as well as having a duty to help each other.
- All Muslims have to follow the Five Pillars, so are equal in their duties to Allah.
- Life is sacred, and belongs to Allah.
- Shari'ah Law applied to life's issues.

Hinduism

- Hindu virtues state:
  - compassion, ahimsa, respect for life (which is sacred)
  - tolerance, support for others, service
  - self-discipline, wisdom, honesty.
- The four stages of life, which each have duties, e.g. householders should have a family.

Using quotations in answers for maximum mark impact

Every year, candidates lose marks because they don't make the best use of the quotations in their answers. If you want to get grade C or better, you need to use them effectively. Let's look at two examples, one from each Unit.

Explain religious attitudes to the issue of abortion. [5]

Christians say do not kill in the commandments. They think life is special because God made it. So they think abortion is wrong. Jews think the same as Christians. They say it breaks the commandments, and that life is special.

This candidate has mentioned teachings from two religions. They needed to spell out what the quotations meant in terms of abortion, like this:

Christians say do not kill in the commandments. They think life is special because God made it. The Old Testament says 'God gives life'. They believe that life is there from conception, so having an abortion is killing and so breaking the commandment. Since there is a life, it is special, and an abortion is like saying it isn't. So they think abortion is wrong.

The answer would be enough to get three marks for Christianity. If the student did the same for Judaism it will easily reach the maximum mark. The way it is written has also made it much clearer and easier for the examiner.

Explain why some religious believers believe that capital punishment is wrong. [4]

In the Bible it says 'do not kill'. It also says that life is sacred. Jesus stopped people stoning a woman.

This gives us three valid ideas, but does not answer the question – the examiner has to make sense of it in terms of capital punishment. Sometimes, the answer isn't obvious enough, and the examiner gives no marks because to them it doesn't answer the question. If you do apply your quotations, you get more marks. A better answer would be:

In the Bible it says 'do not kill'. Obviously, capital punishment is murdering someone even if it is allowed by the government. It also says that life is sacred. This includes people who have done terrible things. Their life is special – what they have done is wrong, so we should deal with that and make them see why it is wrong. Jesus stopped people stoning a woman who had committed adultery; he said no one was innocent, so we should help people see what they have done is wrong, not just kill them. In these teachings, we can see why many Christians think capital punishment is wrong.

The second version does what it needs to. Did you notice that when quotations are applied, the ideas made are also developed so the answers are more detailed? This means higher marks will be awarded.

Command words in the exam – what they are and what they mean

These are the words that instruct you what to do in the exam.
They help you to answer in the way the examiner wants, which gets you more marks!

- **Describe** – give a detailed account of something, as if you are painting a picture using words; it is the same as 'outline'.
- **Explain** – when you make a point, expand it. If the question asks you to explain and you just give a list of ideas, you will not be given more than half the available marks.
- **Explain, using examples** – expand the point(s) you make by giving examples of what you are talking about.
- **Give** – the same as 'write down'; here you can just give a list.
- **How** – is the same as asking 'in what ways', for example 'How do religious people work for animal rights?' is asking 'in what ways' they help animals.
- **Name** – is asking you for an actual technical word or the actual name of something.
- **Refer to ...** – means 'include in your answer', for example you will often be asked to refer to religious beliefs and teachings, so you have to include some to get good marks.
- **What is meant by ...** – you need to say what something means.
- **Why** – give reasons for something, for example why people choose to have children.
- **Do you agree? Give reasons for your answer** – you only get marks for saying why people agree and why they disagree, so make sure you do both. You also need to give explanations to the points you make.
- **... showing that you have thought about more than one point of view** – you have to say why people agree and why people disagree, whatever you yourself think.
- **What do you think? Explain your opinion** – this is asking you to give your own opinion on something, but the statement that is given will always make you think about religion.

How examiners mark your work – introducing AO1 and AO2

The exam has two types of questions – AO1 questions and AO2 questions. The exam paper has equal weighting of these two types.

AO1 (Assessment Objective 1) questions

These are questions that test your *knowledge and understanding* of the course details, and your ability to *apply ideas*. These questions are usually asking for explanations, descriptions and definitions. They also ask for religious attitudes. Marks per question can vary from one to six in any topic – the examiner has to ask two or three questions which together add up to half the total for the topic, i.e. nine marks' worth.

Some examples might be:

Question stem	Life issues	Morality
What is meant by …	… animal rights? [1 mark]	… AID? [1 mark]
Give two ways in which …	… humans damage the environment. [2]	… the elderly can be cared for. [2]
Explain why some religious believers disagree with …	… sexism. [3]	… the use of illegal drugs. [3]
Explain how religious believers could help …	… victims of prejudice. [4]	… young offenders. [4]
Explain religious attitudes to …	… war. [5]	… gambling. [5]

There are grids that examiners use to mark your work. Let's take a look at AO1:

Level Mark	Descriptor	In plain English, that means …
Level 0 0 marks	Nothing correct or relevant.	It is simply wrong!
Level 1 1 mark	Something relevant, which is worthy of a mark.	Just one simple idea; no explanations.
Level 2 2 marks	Elementary knowledge and understanding.	Two ideas here. One idea explained would be fine.
Level 3 3 marks	Sound knowledge and understanding.	You need to give several reasons, and explain some of them. Or you could explain one idea in a lot of detail.
Level 4 4 marks	Clear knowledge and understanding with some development/analysis.	This is a clearly written answer, which flows. It gives ideas, but explains them in good detail as well.
Level 5 5 marks	A detailed answer with some development and/or analysis.	This gives more detail for the examiner to read than Level 4.

AO2 (Assessment Objective 2) questions

These are questions that test your ability to evaluate statements which are linked to the topic you have studied. They are easy to spot – they always start with a statement and then ask you what you think or whether you agree. The 'What do you think?' questions are always worth three marks; the 'Do you agree?' questions are worth six. There is one of each in every topic.

Some examples might be:

- 'Religious people should not have abortions.' What do you think? Explain your opinion. [3 marks]
- 'Genetic modification of anything is playing God.' What do you think? Explain your opinion. [3 marks]
- 'Commitment ceremonies are the most important part of being religious.' What do you think? Explain your opinion. [3 marks]
- 'Religious people should give ten per cent of their wealth to charity.' Do you agree? Give reasons for your answer, showing you have thought about more than one point of view. Refer to religious arguments in your answer. [6 marks]
- 'All zoos should be closed down.' Do you agree? Give reasons for your answer, showing you have thought about more than one point of view. Refer to religious arguments in your answer. [6 marks]
- 'All drugs should be made legal.' Do you agree? Give reasons for your answer, showing you have thought about more than one point of view. Refer to religious arguments in your answer. [6 marks]

Examiners use a grid similar to this for AO2:

Level Mark	Descriptor	Tips
Level 0 0 marks	You give an unsupported opinion, or nothing relevant.	This answer is either restricted to 'I agree/disagree', or is blatantly not answering the question.
Level 1 1 mark	Your opinion is supported by a simple reason.	This is a very short answer, probably makes one point, or two points for two marks.
Level 2 2 marks	Your opinion is supported by two simple reasons (one or both sides).	
Level 3 3 marks	Your opinion is supported by one well-developed reason, or several reasons given across both sides. If there is no religious content, there is a level limit of three marks.	You should be giving three or more ideas, or explaining a couple of ideas to get three marks. You must have some religious stuff in here to get more than three marks. Really you need to be writing in paragraphs, making points and explaining them to get four marks.
Level 4 4 marks	Your opinion is supported by two developed reasons. This can be on the same or different sides.	
Level 5 5 marks	You have explored both sides of the argument through a series of points which are explained in good detail.	You have to write coherently in terms of what you say; it makes good sense. These aren't short answers; they are in paragraphs and show that you really know what the question is getting at and how to challenge it.
Level 6 6 marks	You have explored both sides of the argument through a series of well-explained points, and have applied your knowledge of religion very effectively to support your ideas.	

Your written English

You will be judged on your written English (SPaG – spelling, punctuation and grammar), and given a mark (up to four) for that. This is a simple guide.

0	You wrote nothing; or what you wrote was illegible.
1	You may have written very little, or what you wrote was full of spelling mistakes, grammatical mistakes, and probably not in sentences and paragraphs.
2	There may be quite a few spelling mistakes and/or grammatical errors; simple sentencing; few if any paragraphs used.
3	Few spelling mistakes or grammatical mistakes; use of some technical terms (key words, the proper names for things); good use of sentences and paragraphs.
4	Few if any spelling or grammatical mistakes; good use of technical terms; good use of complicated sentences and paragraphs.

From the start of revision to the exam itself

It's like running a race, really. You do lots of training (that's your revision), you get into the right frame of mind and turn up for the race (that's your last-minute checks and sorting yourself for the exam), and you run the race (the exam itself). The big difference is that only one person can win a race; with GCSEs everyone can win if they do the right preparation.

'Venus told me that champions don't get nervous in tight situations, that helped me a lot. I decided I shouldn't get nervous, just do the best I can'
(Serena Williams)

On your marks ...

Make sure you have all your notes – ensure that no bit of any topic is missing. You can only revise what you have studied already (otherwise it is studying!). Use your class notes to create a set of revision notes. You also have this guide so can add brief notes to what is in here.

Use the revision techniques to fix the information in your head and memory.

Use the sample questions to practise. Go onto the AQA website and download some past papers to practise them. Ask your teacher for more.

Exam tip

AQA's website has past papers and mark schemes on it. Check them out – you can see what questions have come up before, how they have been asked, and what the expected answers were. This helps you see gaps in your knowledge and skills which you can work on.

Get set ...

- Prepare yourself for that exam.
- Get a good sleep the night before.
- Have breakfast (your brain needs fuel). Avoid a stodgy lunch if it is an afternoon exam (or you will be sleepy during it).
- Revision should be light, not in-depth. You are just reminding yourself, so revision postcards with the key points of a topic should be enough.
- Be in good time for the exam – rushing will make you panic.

Go ...

- Sitting in the exam room, breathe slowly and relax yourself (reading every word of the exam paper cover is a good way to calm yourself down). Focus on your space, not the big room you are in. Make sure you can see a clock so you are aware of the time.
- Read the paper, decide which are your best questions. Answer your strongest first to give yourself confidence as starting with your weakest will undermine your confidence and could make you perform less well.
- Take mini-breaks – a few moments between topics to clear your mind so you can focus again. If you panic, take a breathing break to calm yourself down.
- If your mind goes blank on a question just leave it, move on, and come back later. Mark the question paper to remind yourself you need to do that.
- When you have finished, go back over the paper question by question. Check you have done everything the question required. A good method is to read the question, then think of an answer, then read your answer. You are more likely to spot that you have missed something that way.

On the podium ...

The winner's podium for GCSE fits hundreds of thousands. With the right revision, you will be on it and receiving a great grade in the summer.

Religion and Life Issues (AQA B Unit 2 40552)

Topic 1 Religion and animal rights

- How animals help humans.
- How humans use and exploit animals.
- How humans and animals differ.
- Religious attitudes to:
  - animal rights
  - slaughter methods
  - food rules
  - animal experimentation
  - zoos, including their role in conservation of species
  - animals in sport, including hunting, bull fighting and racing
  - farming, including factory farming.
- The 'rights and wrongs' of each of the ways humans use animals.

Topic basics 1: Humans and animals

Are humans and animals equal?

Revised

Yes, because:

- all are created by God
- all live in the same world, and depend on the same resources
- all depend on each other
- they are just different species from the same world.

No, because:

- humans are cleverer
- God gave humans control over animals
- humans have a soul
- the impact of humans is greater so they are not equal
- we can kill animals, but cannot kill other humans.

Key term

Status of animals – the value animals have, e.g. are they as valuable as humans?

Exam tip

The difference between humans and animals is a key core area of this topic. It could be asked in the exam. However, you can bring it into every answer.

How do humans and animals differ?

Revised

- Humans have greater impact on the world around them, e.g. building, clearing land, including potentially destroying it, etc.
- Humans use logic and reasoning to work things out; animals work from instinct.
- Humans have a soul.
- Humans follow moral codes; animals follow nature and instinct.
- Humans communicate in more complex ways, e.g. language.

Animal rights – what do we mean?

Revised

Animals have rights. This means we can't just do what we want with or to animals. **Animal rights** means that animals have the right to be treated properly, fairly and with kindness – even when we intend to kill them. Laws in the UK protect domestic (pet) animals and endangered species. They do this by enforcing the looking after of animals – food, water, shelter and no cruelty. However, many people mistreat animals, both deliberately and through ignorance.

Key term

Animal rights – the rights animals have to live without cruelty, and to have good treatment

Exam tip

Keep your eyes on the news for any useful stories that you can then put into exam answers. They give real examples to illustrate the points you make, for example cases where animals have saved lives of their owners.

Topic basics 2: How humans use animals

Uses of animals – some examples

Revised

- As **pets** (cats, dogs, birds, mice, hamsters, rats, guinea pigs).
- As **exercise** (horses).
- As **helpers** (beasts of burden to move heavy loads or do heavy work – cattle, horses).
- As **work animals** (guide dogs, police dogs, customs dogs, hunting dogs, hunting birds).
- As **providers** (wool from sheep, milk from cows, eggs from hens, honey from bees).
- As **food** (lamb, cows, hens, deer, pigs, fish).
- As **experimental test subjects** (mice, rats, monkeys, dogs).
- As **sport** (bull fighting, horse racing, hunting deer/rabbits/hare/fox).

This isn't an exhaustive list but the uses highlighted here are all you will need for any question. Think about this though. Which uses are good, which are bad? Why?

Animals as companions and helpers

Revised

This includes the pets we have, for example cats and dogs. It also includes guide dogs for the blind and hearing dogs – animals that provide both **companionship** and help to people. Perhaps we can use the term 'friend'.

Key term

Companionship – living with, or keeping someone company, e.g. a pet cat

Key issues

- These animals bring great comfort to humans.
- These animals seem to have a higher status than others.
- These animals seem to have more rights than others because of that status.

Animals as workers or transport

Revised

Animals that work are sometimes called 'beasts of burden' because they do a lot of heavy work as a team with humans. They might be used to transport loads, to plough fields and other farm-related tasks, especially in developing countries. We also now use animals to find explosives and drugs and do a myriad of other work tasks.

Key issues

- Beasts of burden are often worked to death.
- Many of these animals need special training, which can be harsh or at which they fail, so are discarded.
- This is not a natural life for them, and they can be poorly treated, although it can also give them special status, e.g. police dogs.

Farming of animals

Revised

Nearly all the food we eat has come from farms; dairy products, crops and meat. The foods are crucial to our survival. Cheaper meat usually comes from factory farms using battery farming methods. Farms also produce free-range meat (animals allowed to roam free), which is more expensive.

Key issues

- Animals are just treated as products.
- **Farming** means animals live unnatural lives, which can be in cruel conditions.
- Many animals are fattened and killed before they reach adulthood.

> **Key term**
>
> **Farming** – keeping of animals as a foodstock; can be free-range, battery or organic

Animals in hunting

Revised

This is the chasing and killing of animals and birds. **Hunting** could be for food, fur or sport.

Key issues

- Traps used in hunting are cruel, often not killing an animal quickly, and catching unintended victims, e.g. pet dogs.
- Just killing an animal for sport is immoral in many people's eyes – religious or not.
- Some species are being hunted into **extinction**.

> **Key terms**
>
> **Hunting** – the practice of pursuing an animal with the intention to catch and kill it
>
> **Extinction** – where a whole species has been wiped out, so that no more exist, and in the future cannot exist again

Animals in sport

Revised

Animals are used in a variety of sports such as horse and dog racing and blood sports. Blood sports result in injury to the animals, e.g. hunting, hare coursing, dog fighting. All should be regulated within British law. Many people enjoy the thrill of these sports.

Key issues

- Animals that don't make the grade are often slaughtered.
- Most blood sports are very cruel to at least one of the animals, often to the death.

> **Exam tip**
>
> Students often write very generally when asked why religious believers agree or disagree with these uses of animals. This affects marks. Try to be specific in your answers. For example, not all animal experimentation leads to suffering or the death of an animal, but toxicity testing does.

- Treatment of injured animals is often very poor, so they die anyway.
- These sports do not let animals live their natural lives.

Bull fighting is a national sport in Spain in which a matador uses set moves to fight a bull, and eventually kill it.

Key issues

- It is cruel to the bulls.
- The bull dies in great pain over a long period.
- Treatment of fight injuries for 'winning' bulls is poor – many die.

> **Key term**
>
> **Bull fighting** – a sport in which trained matadors fight bulls, usually leading to the death of the bull

Animals in zoos

Revised ☐

Zoos are places that keep animals from all over the world for people to see, both as education and entertainment. Many zoos have breeding programmes that produce animals for other zoos or to return to the wild. This is a crucial conservation role performed by zoos for the future of the world.

> **Key term**
>
> **Zoo** – place where animals are kept for the general public to look at

Key issues

- Animals are rarely in their natural environment or climate.
- Animals have less space than they have in the wild.
- Many zoo animals display clear signs of boredom and distress.

Animal experimentation

Revised ☐

Animal experimentation is when animals are bred deliberately as experiment subjects. Most experiments are to test toxicity (how poisonous something is), medicines and medical techniques. The experiments are for the good of humans. However, most animals are killed during or after the experiment.

> **Key term**
>
> **Animal experimentation** – experiments carried out using animals as the test subject

Key issues

- Animals can suffer greatly in experiments.
- Many experiments seem unnecessary, e.g. to test yet another version of a product that has already been tested, or testing a product in one country that has already been tested in another.
- Animals cannot in any way live natural lives.

> **Exam tip**
>
> Learn a couple of animals that fit into lots of types of uses, so you can reuse them regardless of the question asked, e.g. a dog could be a helper, companion, working animal, used for sport, etc.

Genetic modification and cloning of animals

Revised ☐

Genetic modification involves taking the DNA from an embryo, changing it and putting it back to create a new species of animal, e.g. genetically modifying a pig so that its heart can be used in human organ transplants. **Cloning** is making an exact DNA copy of an animal (e.g. Dolly the sheep).

> **Key terms**
>
> **Genetic modification** – where DNA is taken and adjusted/modified then reinserted into an egg, which is then placed into an animal's womb
>
> **Cloning** – producing an organism exactly identical to another by asexual reproduction, i.e. an exact DNA replica

Key issues

- Many people believe it is morally wrong to do this to animals when we don't know the exact outcomes.
- It costs a lot of money which many people believe could be used more effectively in other ways, e.g. for medical treatment.
- Donor/host animals don't get to live natural lives.

Animals in the fur and ivory trades

The **fur trade** and the **ivory trade** deal in the sale of fur or ivory (elephant tusks). Fur farms are battery farms, which farm as many animals in as small a space as possible to increase profit. The animals they farm for their fur are usually not from that climate, e.g. mink (a cold weather creature) being farmed in Korea (a hot country).

Key issues

- Humans don't need fur as a material in the modern world.
- Elephants are killed simply for their ivory, which is a small part of them.
- Fur farms are very cruel.

Key terms

Fur trade – industry that breeds animals to sell their fur in clothing, etc.

Ivory trade – illegal industry that sells items made from ivory (e.g. elephant tusks)

Exam tip

Some arguments against these uses of animals are common to many animals. Top answers give specific arguments as well, e.g. medical treatment for 'victorious' bulls in bull fights is often so bad, they die anyway.

Exam tip

Most students do better when they practise exam questions, because they develop an effective style and technique. Ask your teacher, or go online, and find some to practise.

Topic basics 3: Treatment of animals and diet

Treatment of animals

At home

- People generally look after pets really well – they are seen as friends.
- There are many laws to protect domesticated animals in the UK.

In the wild

- We put food out for birds, hedgehogs, etc. to help them survive.
- Many species are now endangered because of human lifestyles (e.g. clearing areas for building).
- We ignore most of them, and treat some as vermin, e.g. foxes and rats.

Preventing the extinction of animals

Many animal species are on the verge of extinction (dying out). This is often because of what humans have done. Many zoos try to breed endangered species to try to **preserve species** and therefore prevent extinction. Laws to protect species also exist.

Key terms

Preservation of species – actions taken to keep a species in existence

Stewardship – the belief that humans have a duty to look after the planet, held by all religions

Key issues

- Losing any species is a big blow to the ecosystem.
- Any species we lose is lost to our children – they will inherit a depleted world.
- Moral (and spiritual) guidance is to protect life not destroy it (**stewardship**).

Why are some people vegetarian or vegan?

Revised

A **vegetarian** does not eat meat or fish, while a **vegan** does not eat meat, fish or dairy products. No religion is 100 per cent vegetarian; however, most Sikhs and Hindus and many Buddhists are. This is as a mark of respect for other living beings, either because they have a form of soul, or because they are God's creation.

There are many reasons why non-religious people are vegetarian or vegan, but the most obvious are:

- **medical** problems, like an allergy
- **dislike** of the taste of meat
- **disagreeing with farming methods** or **slaughter methods**
- they think it is **morally wrong** to eat meat
- they were **brought up** that way
- **religious rules**.

Key terms

Vegetarian – a person who does not eat any meat, fish or meat products

Vegan – a person who does not eat any meat, fish, meat products or dairy products

Exam tip

The words in bold give you a simple 'to remember' list for use in the exam, should the question of why people are vegan or vegetarian come up. Learn them!

Food rules and the slaughter of animals

Revised

Many Christians do not eat red meat on Fridays to remember it was the day Jesus died; many choose not to eat any meat at all during Lent.

Judaism has the most complicated set of rules about food – Kashrut, which is based on laws from the Torah. Islam also has specific rules about what is halal (forbidden). In both religions, the rules are mainly about meat. It is fine to eat meat from many animals, but the animal has to have been ritually slaughtered. This means a prayer of thanks is said before the kill; then, the animal is killed by having its throat slit, so that its blood is released. There may be prayers afterwards. Any remaining blood is also drawn from the meat. Neither religion allows meat from a pig to be eaten.

Other religions might not have a precise process, but would expect animals to be humanely killed.

Common mistakes

Revised

Candidates often mix up religions when they write about rules or attitudes, for example writing about Islam believing in reincarnation of animals. Although you will get some marks, you won't get many. Make sure you know the right stuff for the right religions.

Religious teachings on religion and animal rights: good teachings to learn

Revised

Sikhism

- If you say there is God in every being, why kill a chicken (Guru Granth Sahib)?
- God's light is in every creature (Guru Granth Sahib).
- Many Sikhs are vegetarian out of respect for God's creation and the langar serves only vegetarian food.
- All food is pure as God has given it for our sustenance (Adi Granth).
- Guru Gobind Singh stated that he enjoyed hunting – so it's not forbidden.

Buddhism

- The First Precept is to not harm other sentient beings.
- Right Livelihood – to have no job that exploits animals.
- All living things fear being put to death – let no one kill or cause others to kill (Dhammapada).
- Bodhisattva vow: 'as long as sentient beings suffer, I will be around to help'.
- The Buddha gave up his life in many lifetimes to help animals.
- Many Buddhists are vegetarian out of respect for all living beings.

Christianity

- God made the world and gave humans dominion over it (Genesis).
- Animals are part of creation and deserve respect and protection (Assisi Declarations).
- The Earth and everything in it is the Lord's (Genesis).
- Jesus said God cares about even the sparrows.
- Scientists must abandon laboratories and factories of death (Pope John Paul II).
- Many Christians do not eat red meat on Fridays to remember Jesus' death on Good Friday.
- Many Christians eat no meat at all during Lent.

All religions teach:
- stewardship
- sanctity of life
- companionship

Judaism

- G-d made the world and all in it.
- A righteous man looks after his animals.
- Do not be cruel to animals (Naochide Laws).
- Animals must be respected as they are G-d's creation but human life is always more important.
- Do not work on the Sabbath – nor your animals (Torah).
- Jews must follow Kashrut – laws relating to the food they may or may not eat and its preparation, which come from the Torah.

Islam

- Humans are Khalifah – trustees (stewards) of the world.
- Nature is inferior to humans and can be used to improve the well-being of people.
- Showing kindness to an animal is an act rewarded by Allah.
- Muhammad (pbuh) insisted animals were well treated.
- If a man unjustly kills an animal he will be accused by the animal on Judgement Day.
- Muslims should only eat halal meat – that which has been ritually slaughtered.

Hinduism

- Avoid harming all forms of life (ahimsa).
- Hindu worship includes respect for all and many deities are linked to specific animals.
- By avoiding harm to animals, humans will come to be ready for eternal life (Laws of Manu).
- It is the duty of the householder to feed animals.
- 'On a Brahmin…cow … elephant…dog…wise men look with an equal eye' (Bhagavad Gita).
- Many Hindus are vegetarian to show respect to God's creation.

Common mistakes

Candidates often use teachings such as 'Do not kill' and 'Love your neighbour' for this topic. Don't. They are both about humans, not animals!

Revised

Key term

Sanctity of life – the belief that life is special or sacred

What questions on this topic look like:
Religion and animal rights

This page contains a range of examples of questions that could be on an exam paper for this topic. Practise them all to strengthen your knowledge and technique while revising. Check the website for answers to some of these, with tips. Check back to pages 11–12 to see the marking grids that examiners use: this will help you mark your answers.

1   What is meant by animal rights? [1]
2   What is meant by vegetarian? [1]
3   Explain what is meant by animal rights. [2]
4   Give **two** ways in which humans use animals. [2]
5   Explain why some religious believers think it is wrong to eat meat. [3]
6   Explain how humans and animals are different. [3]
7   'Animals should have the same rights as humans.' What do you think? Explain your opinion. [3]
8   Explain religious attitudes to animals. Refer to beliefs and teachings in your answer. [4]
9   Explain **two** ways in which religious people can work for animal rights. [4]
10 Explain religious attitudes to experiments on live animals. You may refer to religious beliefs and teachings in your answer. [4]
11 Explain religious attitudes to using animals in farming. Refer to religious beliefs and teachings in your answer. [5]
12 Explain the ways in which humans make use of animals in the world today. [5]
13 Describe the food laws that religious believers might follow. [5]
14 'Religious believers should support animal experimentation.' Do you agree? Explain your reasons, showing you have thought about more than one point of view. Refer to religious arguments in your answer. [6]
15 'Zoos should all be closed down.' Do you agree? Explain your reasons, showing you have thought about more than one point of view. Refer to religious arguments in your answer. [6]
16 'It is wrong to use animals in sport.' Do you agree? Explain your reasons showing you have thought about more than one point of view. Refer to religious arguments in your answer. [6]

Online

Exam tip

- Remember you only need to look at the religion(s) you have been taught, but learn at least one specific one to go with your general teachings.
- Remember to APPLY the teaching to the question after you have stated it – see how simple this is by referring to page 9.
- For most answers probably three specific teachings plus the generic ones will be sufficient.

Did you know that F-grade candidates rarely use the correct technical terms in their exam? This means they can find some questions difficult because they just didn't know what the question was asking. If this sounds like you, make a list of words that are important, and make sure you learn them all.

Did you know that C-grade candidates use some of the technical words in their exam, but not as many as they could do? They might recognise the words when they are in the questions, but they don't answer with enough depth. Using the words makes your answers sound better, and usually means you will be sharper in what you are saying. Learn the words, and use them more, so that they are part of your vocabulary anyway.

Did you know that A-grade candidates know and use the correct technical language all the time in their exam? This makes the exam easier because they don't have to try to work out what the questions are asking. It makes their answers better, because they are sharper, sounding more knowledgeable. If this is you, add greater depth to your use of these words. Don't be satisfied with just knowing what they mean, learn examples and find out more detail about each one.

Which one are you? And how do you move to the next level?

Topic 2 Religion and planet Earth

- How the world and life began.
- The planet as a source of awe and wonder.
- How and why people damage the environment.
- How and why individuals help the environment.
- The world's response to environmental problems.
- Religious attitudes to:

  o the natural world
  o climate change
  o pollution
  o use and abuse of natural resources
  o destruction and conservation of natural habitat.

- Environmental problems caused by modern lifestyles, and potential solutions.

Topic basics 1: The origins of life

This topic is about the planet we live on so a good place to start is 'Where did it come from?' You need to learn the scientific and the religious ideas and arguments for and against them.

Science: The Big Bang
Revised

- **Twenty billion years ago** – 'there was nothing'.
- **A huge explosion** caused a cloud of dust and gas.
- Cloud settled to **form the universe and the planets in it**.
- Earth was only mud – primeval soup.
- Proteins and acids in the mud fused together.
- Simple life forms began.
- Life developed into insects, birds, fish, reptiles and mammals.
- Five million years ago – the first human.

Exam tip

You are unlikely to be asked more than a two-mark question on the scientific origins of the universe. Learn the key aspects, which are in bold, and you will get full marks.

God and nature
Revised

Religions use the following ideas to support their belief in creation:

- The beauty, complexity, power, yet peace and calm of the world cannot be an accident, suggesting a creator – God.
- The world's design seems deliberate – so it must have a designer.
- How did it happen? Science can't explain why something that began with nothing suddenly became a place with the right conditions for life.
- The more you look at the beauty of the world – the sea's power, landscapes, the planets, sunsets, etc – the more filled with **awe and wonder** and questions you are.
- There seems to be no other explanation for the world other than that God made it exist.
- We must therefore respect this gift and worship God by looking after it.

Key term

Awe and wonder – sense of respect and admiration, often linked with fear (e.g. fear of the power of God which is being demonstrated)

Creation

Christianity, Islam and Judaism have the same story:

- God created the world from nothing in six 'days'.
- Firstly the world: air, water, land vegetation, sun, moon, stars and seasons.
- Then life: birds, fish and animals ... finally humans.
- On the seventh day God rested, he was pleased and the world was good.

Hinduism believes that:

- Vishnu slept on a cobra in the middle of nothingness.
- Vishnu wakes and a lotus flower grows from his navel.
- Brahma is inside the lotus. He creates the world.
- Shiva is also there to be responsible for the cycle of life and death.

Sikhism teaches that:

- God created the world.
- Without God nothing exists.
- God keeps life going.

> **Exam tip**
>
> You need only write from one religion, but if you know information from two it is easier to give better answers, as you know a broader range of information. So, for example, it would be difficult to use only one religion's idea of creation and get four marks; learning two of them makes it easy to get all four.

Stewardship and the future

- The world belongs to God so we have a duty to look after it. This is called **stewardship**.
- Looking after the world shows respect and gratitude and it is a duty to keep.
- It is like an act of worship to look after God's world.
- If I ruin the world I have to live in the mess.
- ...So do others and our children...
- God will reward me if I look after his world, but punish me if I don't.
- Hindus, Buddhists and Sikhs believe in reincarnation and that they will need the world again!

> **Key term**
>
> **Stewardship** – sense of responsibility for the planet, for animals, for others; a duty to look after

Topic basics 2: The Earth's problems

There are a number of problems and issues that affect the Earth which you need to be aware of as well as some of the solutions to these problems. There are also some extra technical terms here that you need to know.

> **Exam tip**
>
> For the exam, be able to say what the specific issue is, for example global warming: why it is happening; problems raised by it; and possible solutions.

Pollution is where too much of something has caused an imbalance and damage to the environment. It is something (often a dangerous substance) usually dumped into water, onto land or released into the air. Some examples include:

- **acid rain** (rain made acidic because of air pollution from factories and power stations) which damages buildings
- **oil spills** from tankers that kill birds and sea life
- **toxic chemicals** spilled into rivers and on land, sometimes caused by a build-up of pesticides from farms.

> **Key term**
>
> **Pollution** – excess of anything, which leads to environmental problems, e.g. an oil spillage leads to pollution in the sea, which kills sea-dwelling life forms

Problems

- Rivers and waterways become contaminated – fish die or we eat them and the poisons are passed on to us.
- Land is covered with litter and landfill dumping sites.
- Air is polluted by factories, cars, noise – this affects human health.
- Beaches and the sea are polluted with sewage.

Solutions

- Cut the level of toxic waste.
- **Recycle** rubbish.
- Use cars and planes less often, and use cleaner fuels.
- Governments can make world agreements and enforce them.
- Use of cleaner fuels, e.g. for heating and cooking.

> **Key term**
>
> Recycling – reusing something rather than just letting it become waste

Global warming
Revised

'Climate change' is another phrase for this because **global warming** is leading to climate change. Scientists tell us that the Earth's temperature is getting hotter because greenhouse gases are allowing the Sun's rays into our atmosphere but then trap them. This can have dire consequences for humans, animals and the natural world on Earth and under the sea.

Effects and problems caused

- Ice caps melting cause the seas to rise and land to disappear under the sea.
- As oceans get warmer, the water expands and sea levels rise, drowning coastlines and flooding coastal settlements.
- **Severe weather** patterns – floods and droughts – lead to destruction of crops and **famine**.
- Sea life and reefs die as sea temperature and depth changes make the conditions wrong for the life in those areas.
- Animals' habitats are destroyed as climatic change happens, e.g. polar bears are now threatened because the ice flows they need to travel on are disappearing.
- Cancers are on the increase because more of the harmful rays from the Sun are getting through the atmosphere to our level.

Solutions

- Using less energy, for example through insulating our houses, switching off appliances, etc.
- Industries finding alternative and renewable energy sources.
- Creating more renewable energy sources with low-carbon emissions, such as wind farms, and harnessing wave and solar energy.
- Creating less pollution through recycling more, using our cars less, reducing factory emissions, etc.
- Everyone – individuals, companies, and governments – taking responsibility for being part of the solution, including setting and hitting targets.

> **Key terms**
>
> **Global warming** – the heating up of the Earth's atmosphere, leading to climatic change
>
> **Severe weather** – weather conditions that are extreme and not usual for the area, e.g. flooding, drought
>
> **Famine** – extreme scarcity of food, often because of the failure of harvests due to weather conditions

> **Exam tip**
>
> Learn all these types of issues. Questions can be asked specifically about any of them. If you don't know what 'global warming' is you can't get the four marks for the question 'Explain how religious believers could fight global warming'

> **Common mistakes**
>
> Candidates think they can get great marks from having a very general knowledge of the subject. They can't. You need to know more than God created the world, life is sacred and 'love your neighbour' to get the higher levels of marks.
>
> Revised

Destruction of natural habitats

The **destruction of natural habitats** is being caused by pollution and by direct human activity. **Deforestation** is an example of this. It is the removal of rainforests at a dramatic speed for other purposes, for example for building, mining and cattle grazing. The intention may not be to get rid of all the species that inhabit an area, but that is definitely the result. This is happening everywhere that humans live, farm or build.

Issues

- Animals die and species can become extinct because their homes disappear.
- Rainforests contain many plant species that we can use in new medicines and these will be lost.
- Trees are good for the environment. They capture the carbon dioxide from the atmosphere and produce oxygen for us to breathe.

Solutions

- We have to balance humans' needs for land with our use of the environment, because when trees or species have gone they can't return.
- International agreements to protect areas – creating national parks, for example.

Key terms

Destruction of natural habitat – actions that lead to the natural homes of plants and animals being destroyed, often leading to the deaths of those species

Deforestation – cutting down trees over extensive areas

Exam tip

Think what religious believers' attitudes should be to any of these issues. If you have already thought about them, you have more chance of answering a specific question well if it comes up in the exam, e.g. 'Explain religious attitudes to the abuse of natural resources'.

Use and abuse of natural resources

Natural resources include vegetation, minerals and fossil fuels such as coal, gas and oil. Humans use fossil fuels very heavily. Think how much we rely on coal, gas and oil for travel, heating and energy. So what are the problems, and what are the potential solutions?

Issues

- Fossil fuels are being used in greater amounts and at a faster rate.
- Increasing use of technology across more of the world means more use of energy and resources, which causes more pollution.
- A greater number of people travel more and further, using up more fuel and creating pollution.
- Natural resources such as coal and oil are running out because of the rate at which they are used. The Earth took millions of years to produce them. We need to find other sources of energy that won't run out – and we need to switch to them.
- When oil runs out the world would cease to work as it does at the moment because we rely too heavily on it as a fuel and haven't set up alternatives in enough quantity.

Solutions

- To cut down on energy use.
- To create renewable energy such as wind power, solar power, wave energy – and things we don't even know about yet.
- To stop cutting down rainforest.
- To fertilise and reuse cleared areas, rather than just moving onto another patch, spoiling that as well.

Key term

Natural resources – the things we use that occur naturally, e.g. gas, oil, coal, wood

Exam tip

Learn each one of these issues – you will have met most in Science or Geography. You need to be able to answer questions about each, and you can't do that if you don't know what they are!

Modern living

It is easy to think that global warming and pollution are not our fault or are issues too big for us to deal with, but as individuals we put huge demands on the planet. We have to accept that modern lifestyles put a big demand on the Earth and its resources – fuel demands for all the technologies we use and for our travel; food we buy and waste; rubbish sites filling up, and so on. We have to think of the effect of the following issues, but also realise we are both the problem and the solution. We can make a difference – we just have to try.

Check out 'extreme recycling' on the web for examples of people making a difference.

Issues

- We have cars that produce polluting gases.
- We produce tons of rubbish as a family each year – food waste, packaging and so on.
- We use a great deal of energy, often without care.
- Most of our foods are grown with pesticides and these poison the land.
- A lot of fast food comes from cattle grazed on land that was rainforest, which was cleared to grow animal food used round the world to produce the meat that we all eat.

Solutions

- Take responsibility for our own contribution. If everyone did a little then collectively it would have a great effect. If we walk more, recycle, turn off lights, take things off standby, eat organic food, etc. we can reduce our individual 'carbon footprint', i.e. the amount of carbon we are each responsible for.

How people can help

What about … you?

Individuals could:

- make small changes to their lifestyle to save energy
- adopt animals in nature reserves
- recycle more
- join an environmental organisation – Greenpeace, for example
- protest against organisations that damage the environment.

… religious believers?

Religious believers could:

- do the same things that individuals do
- make sure their place of worship is as environmentally friendly as possible, for example recycling, etc.
- deliver sermons about good stewardship of the planet
- have recycling bins on the grounds of the building
- group together to lobby for change
- support environmental charities en masse
- protest as a group
- pray for guidance.

> **Exam tip**
>
> When asked what religious believers could do about something, make sure you get at least one obviously religious way in there – like praying (for guidance or help).

> **Exam tip**
>
> Remember this is a Religious Studies exam. If asked about the issues caused by any of these specific problems, could you think of any attitudes religious people might have? For example, would religious people think that deforestation goes against the belief that we should thank God for His creation?

Topic basics 3: Looking after the world

The work being done to look after the world includes international action such as Earth Summits, targets to reduce carbon emissions, action involving sustainable development, and conservation projects.

Exam tip

You could be asked about what individuals could do, or what groups could do, or about a specific way of helping, like the Earth Summits. Learn something concrete for each so you can answer them all.

International efforts
Revised

Earth Summits

Earth Summits are meetings of governments from all over the world every ten years to discuss environmental issues. These summits make efforts to build agreements between nations. They look at environmental problems and particularly try to help poorer countries to tackle the issues, as these countries have little money, but need to develop quickly for the benefit of their people. Quick development with little money is usually very destructive for the environment.

Target setting – Kyoto

In 2002 at the Earth Summit in Kyoto, Japan, many governments agreed to sign up to set targets for the future in order to:

- use cleaner power more – wind, solar, wave energies
- reduce the amount of carbon dioxide emissions
- allow richer countries to 'buy' quotas of carbon emissions from countries that do not fully use their own quota, which would help the economies of those countries.

If these agreements are kept they will have a positive impact on reducing global warming, because actions make the difference, not just agreements.

Sustainable development

Sustainable development is at the heart of the Earth Summits and all the agreements made at them. Governments have to find technological advances and energies that can still exist and benefit people of future generations. It is no good swapping one resource that will run out for another one that will also run out. It is wrong to use up all the resources and leave nothing for the future. It is also wrong to expect the poorest countries to pay the highest prices to make life better for their people now – they need to be helped by the richer countries.

Conservation

Conservation is the idea of protecting an area or species. It could be action to repair a damaged area, such as planting trees, or to protect an area such as starting up nature reserves, etc.

Conservation can be the work of governments (e.g. setting up protected areas), organisations (e.g. doing large-scale tree-planting projects) or individuals (such as taking a holiday to work for an environmental project).

Key terms

Earth Summit – meeting between representatives of governments from all over the world to try to reach agreements about what can be done to look after the planet

Sustainable development – projects that can continue, without being replaced or replenished

Conservation – looking after, preservation of the natural environment

Exam tip

Researching to find specific examples to use is a good source of information for the exam. Try to find out about a religious organisation and what they do, then you can answer any organisation question, but you could also answer for an individual (as they may join that organisation, whose work then becomes their own).

Topic basics 4: Religious attitudes to planet Earth

Religious attitudes to planet Earth

Revised

Buddhism

- Buddhists believe that all life should be respected and as we will use the Earth during many lifetimes it makes sense that we should all look after it. We protect it for ourselves as well as our children.
- Buddhists believe that it is ignorance and greed that lead to most of the pollution being caused – companies building factories in the third world so they can pay the workers less, have fewer pollution controls to follow and make bigger profits. Ignorance and greed also stop people from reaching enlightenment – so it's double damage!!
- We must look after the world for our own karmic sakes, as well as for the well-being of the planet and all other inhabitants.

Hinduism

- Brahman is in all life, so we should respect all life.
- Hindu life began many years ago and was linked to a simple existence living on the land. The ideas of sanctity of life and non-violence became built into the religion.
- All life is interdependent – plants and animals and all life depend on their environment so everyone needs to protect it. All souls will be reborn so we need to return to Earth again and if God is in all nature then we show an act of worship by looking after it.

Christianity

- God created the world. It was a 'good' creation, which was perfection at its making.
- God gave us the world and the responsibility to look after it. Many Christians actively campaign to 'heal the world' as the Earth is a great gift that God has entrusted us with.
- We also have a responsibility to each other, the poor of the world and our future children to make sure the world is still intact for many generations to come.
- 'Loving your neighbour' means not destroying the world.

Judaism

- After creating the world G-d gave us the duty of stewardship. We should respect G-d's creation.
- It has always been part of Jewish mitzvoth to leave land fallow in a regular cycle.
- Tikkun olam (repairing the world) is interpreted as tackling environmental issues; tzedek (justice) means justice for all animals and the world itself.
- To 'love your neighbour' you have to not wreck the world.

Islam

- The world is the work of Allah.
- Humans are Khalifahs – trustees of Allah's world. Allah knows who damages his creation and punishment will follow on Judgement Day.
- It is an act of worship to look after the world.
- The idea of the Ummah means we have a duty to pass on the world to the next generations in good condition.

Sikhism

- The world is a gift from God – it only exists because God wants it to. Sikhs believe in evolution, and that God has created the universe many times over.
- Sikhs perform Sewa for others so safeguarding the world is essential. For example, if we help the world's poor we help the environment.
- The Gurus said God is within everything so damage the world – damage God.

Exam tip

Remember you only need to learn the teaching(s) from the religion(s) you have studied.

Exam tip

Work out how each of these applies to each specific issue, or makes people act for change. If you think about it, and write some ideas about your thoughts, you will be better prepared for the exam.

Buddhism

- The First Precept is to not harm.
- Conservation is about our own survival not just about morality (Dalai Lama).
- The Earth is not just our heritage but our ultimate source of life (Dalai Lama).
- Destruction of nature results from greed, ignorance and a lack of respect for the Earth's living things – this shows a lack of respect to future generations (Dalai Lama).
- Compassion should be the centre of all actions.

Sikhism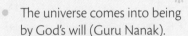

- The universe comes into being by God's will (Guru Nanak).
- In nature we see God and in nature we hear God (Adi Granth).
- God created everything (Guru Nanak).
- Respect for all life.
- The Sikh ideal is a simple life free from waste.

Christianity ✚

- God made the world – humans are stewards of it (Genesis).
- The Earth is the Lord's (Psalms).
- More than ever people are responsible for the planet's future (Pope John Paul II).
- Jesus said love your neighbour.
- Respect for life extends to all of creation (Pope John Paul II).

All religions teach:
- creation
- stewardship
- awe
- community
- conservation

Judaism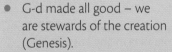

- G-d made all good – we are stewards of the creation (Genesis).
- The Torah speaks of not wasting, so we should conserve resources.
- The Earth and everything in it is the Lord's (Ketuvim).
- All I created for you. Do not corrupt or desolate my world, there will be no repair to it (Midrash Ecclesiastes Rabbah).
- Love your neighbour as yourself (Leviticus).

Islam ☾★

- The world is green and beautiful – Allah made you Khalifahs over it (Qur'an).
- The world was created as a place of worship (Qur'an).
- The Earth has been created as a mosque (Hadith).
- Muhammad (pbuh) gave the example of not wasting nature – water was his example.
- Even on Doomsday a palm shoot should still be planted (Hadith).

Hinduism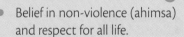

- Belief in non-violence (ahimsa) and respect for all life.
- Hindus should focus on environmental issues (Artharva Veda).
- Trees give fuel, shade, a resting place, shelter to birds and medicines – this is their daily sacrifice (Varaha Purana).
- All life is interdependent – humans, animals and plants.

Exam practice

What questions on this topic look like:
Religion and planet Earth

Check back to pages 11–12 to see the grids examiners use to help you mark your answers.

This page contains a range of examples of questions that could be on an exam paper for this topic. Practise them all to strengthen your knowledge and technique while revising. Check the website for answers to some of these, with tips.

1   What is meant by pollution? [1]

2   What is meant by stewardship? [1]

3   Explain what is meant by global warming. [2]

4   Give **two** ways in which humans damage the world. [2]

5   Explain why some religious believers think it is wrong to destroy the natural environment. [3]

6   Explain how humans can look after the world. [3]

7   'Damaging the world is disrespectful to God.' What do you think? Explain your opinion. [3]

8   Explain religious attitudes to the use of natural resources. Refer to beliefs and teachings in your answer. [4]

9   Explain **two** ways in which religious people can work for the conservation of the planet. [4]

10 Explain religious attitudes to the environment. Use religious beliefs and teachings in your answer. [4]

11 Explain religious attitudes to destruction of the environment. Refer to religious beliefs and teachings in your answer. [5]

12 Explain the ways in which governments have worked to help the planet. [5]

13 Describe the ways in which modern living is putting pressure on the environment. [5]

14 'Humans should respect the world because God created it.' Do you agree? Explain your reasons, showing you have thought about more than one point of view. Refer to religious arguments in your answer. [6]

15 'Climate change is the biggest problem for humans.' Do you agree? Explain your reasons, showing you have thought about more than one point of view. Refer to religious arguments in your answer. [6]

16 'Religious people should do the most to look after the planet.' Do you agree? Explain your reasons, showing you have thought about more than one point of view. Refer to religious arguments in your answer. [6]

Online

Exam tip

Did you know that F-grade candidates usually write very little. They usually only give one idea in any answer. They only know a bit of everything they need to know. If this is you, make sure you double the numbers of points you make in each answer.

Did you know that C-grade candidates write quite a lot, but often do not clearly make their points. They usually don't consistently explain themselves – sometimes they do, sometimes they don't. They know quite a lot about the subject, but not the details. By knowing the information in depth, you can improve this.

Did you know that A-grade candidates write lots. They explain most of the points they make. They use lots of the religious words for things. They obviously know their stuff really well.

So, which are you?

Topic 3 Religion and prejudice

Key knowledge

- Different types of prejudice and examples of each.
- Why people are prejudiced, and how they show it.
- Relevance of tolerance, justice, harmony and the value of each person.
- Religious attitudes to prejudice.
- Religious attitudes to:
  - racism
  - sexism
  - homophobia
  - ageism
  - religious prejudice.
- How religions help the victims of prejudice and discrimination.
- What specific individuals have done to fight prejudice.
- What pressure groups and the government have done, e.g. the Race Relations Act.

Topic basics 1: What are prejudice and discrimination?

The exam often asks about what key words mean, such as **prejudice**, **discrimination** and **racism**. It also often asks why people become prejudiced, and how they show it. This topic basic tries to tackle those questions.

Key terms

Prejudice – pre-judge someone without evidence (negative thought)

Discrimination – putting prejudicial thoughts into action

Racism – discrimination on the grounds of colour of skin (race)

Types of prejudice   Revised

There are many different types of prejudice, and some are focused on in the exam:

- Racism, e.g. calling someone names because of the colour of their skin.
- **Sexism**, e.g. refusing someone a job because of their gender.
- **Ageism**, e.g. not listening to someone's opinion because of their age.
- **Homophobia**, e.g. someone being attacked because the attacker thinks they are gay.
- **Religious prejudice**, e.g. killing people of a certain faith because of what they believe.

Key terms

Sexism – discrimination on the grounds of being male or female (gender or sex)

Ageism – discrimination on the grounds of being old, middle aged or young (age)

Homophobia – discrimination on the grounds of sexuality (gay or lesbian)

Religious prejudice – discrimination on the grounds of faith or belief

Common mistakes   Revised

Candidates mix up 'Why' and 'How' questions so read questions carefully. 'How religious believers fight prejudice' is not the same as 'why' they do.

Exam tip

Learn the definition of each of these and an example of it in action. This will help you answer one-, two-, or three-mark AO1 questions.

Causes of prejudice

Revised

Here are some of the main causes of prejudice:

- Upbringing – parents' attitudes against a certain group are also believed by their children, so that the children behave in an unfair way towards that group of people.
- Bad experience – a bad experience with someone from a certain group may affect a person's attitudes to others in the same group, leading to the belief 'They are all like that'.
- Media – biased coverage of an event may make someone form prejudiced attitudes, because they believe what the media said and take it as true for everyone in that group.
- Ignorance – judging someone or a group of people in a negative way without having any actual real knowledge about them.
- Scapegoating – blaming others as an excuse for a problem, e.g. Hitler blaming the Jews for economic problems in Germany before the Second World War.

> **Exam tip**
> Learn to list each cause, say what they mean and give an example.

How discrimination is shown

Revised

Discrimination can be shown in many ways, such as:

- verbal, e.g. making a discriminatory comment or a joke, etc
- physical, e.g. violent action towards a person, even to the point of murder
- abuse of property, e.g. negative graffiti slogans
- discrimination by action, e.g. not employing someone, shunning someone or bullying.

Effects of discrimination

Revised

Discrimination can affect people and society in different ways, such as:

Negative

- Emotional – feeling left out, lonely, different, depressed or suicidal.
- Isolation within a **community**.
- Physically driven out of a community.
- Sense of total injustice.
- Loss of property or possessions.
- Actual death, as the most extreme form of discrimination is murder.

> **Key term**
> **Community** – people who work or live together so that everyone benefits

Positive

- Feelings of determination, not giving in, proud of who they are.
- Sense of community as people fight together against discrimination.
- Sense of purpose.
- Can provide jobs and support to people under-represented in areas of society, e.g. positive recruitment drive for homosexual people in the police force.
- Balancing up society, for example making sure that all groups are fairly treated and represented in all aspects of society.

> **Exam tip**
> For any questions on this topic, it is good to know examples. For example, if asked for causes of prejudice, give the cause and an example.

Topic basics 2: Attitudes to the key types of prejudice

Racism

Racism is **illegal** in the UK (**2000 Race Relations Amendment Act**). All religions believe it is **wrong to discriminate** because of colour/race.

Holy books and leaders teach **respect**, **harmony** and **tolerance** of each other; they believe that all people are **equal**. However, racism still exists and religious believers should **fight against it**.

> ### Exam tip
> Remember to learn the key concepts:
> - justice
> - tolerance
> - community
> - harmony.
>
> You might be asked to apply them to specific prejudices, e.g. 'How might religious believers work for justice in cases of discrimination?' You can always use them in any of your answers to show the examiner you really understand the topic, e.g. 'Religious people show tolerance to those of other faiths'.

> ### Key terms
> **Race Relations Act** – law making discrimination illegal
>
> **Harmony** – to live peacefully with understanding and respect
>
> **Tolerance** – to accept people's differences

Ageism
Revised ☐

The **law is NOT ageist** – age limits are set for our own good. For example, an age is set before which people are not allowed to marry so that they will be old enough to make such a decision properly. However, **ageism can affect anyone** at any time – young and old people suffer from it.

Holy books teach that **parents and the elderly** should be respected – they are **wise and experienced** so need to be listened to, and we have a **duty** to look after them.

Young people are the **future** and their views should be valued.

> ### Exam tip
> The exam can ask you about attitudes to any of these specific types of prejudice, so you need to learn all of them. In each section, the key words and phrases to learn are in bold to make it easier to know what to use in the exam to impress the examiner!

Sexism
Revised ☐

Sexism **mainly affects women**, who suffer from discrimination which comes from traditional practices. Religions state that everyone is **equal**. In some religious traditions women are **prevented from taking on leadership**, which some people regard as sexist. The **1975 Sex Discrimination Act** gives legal protection to both sexes.

Role of women

Are **restrictions on women** in religions really discrimination? Men do have **more rights, freedoms and choices** than women. However, as long as women are **happy in their roles** then we cannot label it discrimination.

When women are **not able to lead, but want to**, then there is a problem. It is argued that women could offer a **different approach** from men, and they should be able to **serve God** at the **highest level**.

Homophobia

Attitudes to this are **different** to other forms of prejudice. Gay people often receive **little support** from religions and families.

All religions believe it is **wrong to be homophobic** – gay men and lesbians should not be targeted, which is **against UK law** anyway. However, they mainly agree that it is **wrong to have homosexual relationships** as they are seen as **unnatural** and against the reasons for sex – they cannot produce children. Many **Holy Books condemn** homosexuality.

Things are changing though with the Gay Church Movement, and legally, e.g. the **2007 Sexual Orientation Act**, plus civil partnerships, pension rights, etc.

Disability

Everyone is equal – **God creates us in different ways**, and **values us despite our differences**.

People with disabilities can actually teach us many things about attitudes to life. Difficulties can be overcome, and most people with a disability **live full and fulfilling lives**. We should not try to judge the **quality of life** of another. The **2005 Disability Act** makes this discrimination illegal; all religions would support this.

Religious prejudice

Each religion declares it has the right way so there is potential for discrimination in that 'being right' can make you feel superior, and can mean you look down on others who aren't the same. Many wars and wholesale persecutions have been because of religious prejudice, e.g. the Crusader wars against Muslims; Hitler's persecution of the Jews in the Holocaust; Catholic Christian persecution of Muslims in Yugoslavia; Muslim persecution of Christians in Iraq.

- People are free to practise their own religion within Britain, so the law protects them.
- It is against the law to discriminate because of religious symbols, clothing and actions. Generally religious people support this stance.
- Organisations have been able to ban the wearing of religious insignia where it is not a required part of the religion, e.g. British Airways banning Christians from wearing visible crosses while on duty.
- Most religious groups promote tolerance of others, because they promote peace and understanding of others.
- For some religious people, different religions are seen as being different ways to the same goal.
- Religious groups often argue with and against other religious groups, and violent clashes are in the news regularly, e.g. Hindus and Muslims fighting each other in India. There can also be arguments within religions, e.g. the Catholic and Protestant arguments in Northern Ireland in the last century.

Exam tip

In the twentieth century, there were many examples of religious prejudice carried out in an extreme form. Do a little research about the Holocaust or the Bosnian War to give you good examples to use in the exam.

Looks and lifestyle

Revised

Although not a specific prejudice, looks and lifestyle are things that people find lead to discrimination against them often. An extreme example is that of Sophie Lancaster, a young woman who was murdered simply because of how she looked.

- We should not be too eager to judge just on looks.
- It is character not looks that matters.
- People should always be given a chance.
- Religions might not agree with certain lifestyles but they are not in a position to discriminate.
- Help, understanding, tolerance and respect should be shown.

> **Exam tip**
>
> Check out the website in memory of Sophie Lancaster to give you information about what charities do. www.sophielancasterfoundation.com

Topic basics 3: Responding to prejudice

Positive discrimination

Revised

Positive discrimination is where people are given chances, jobs and roles precisely because they belong to a group that is usually in the **minority**, under-represented or victims of prejudice. Sometimes it is necessary to consider what people can offer that is different from the current workforce in terms of attitudes, experience and skills, particularly if everyone who applies for the job or role has the same qualifications.

- This helps to even situations out, so that all groups are represented in any organisation.
- It gives opportunities to those who are usually discriminated against.
- It can make groups or organisations more representative of society, e.g. recruiting gay officers to the police force.
- It challenges prejudice by putting those usually discriminated against into jobs or roles.

> **Key terms**
>
> **Positive discrimination** – benefits given to those who usually face negative discrimination
>
> **Minority** – a small group often discriminated against by larger groups

How organisations respond to prejudice and victims of it

Revised

Of course, organisations raise money and awareness. The money is needed to pay for the work they do, as well as to support victims. The awareness is because most people are unaware of the full impact of prejudice, or need to know more to stop them from being prejudiced. Political lobbying and research help organisations to get laws changed and make our society fairer.

There are many very well-known groups, some of which are listed below. Check out their websites to give yourself a good understanding of problems and their solutions and work.

- **Hope not hate** is an organisation that links local anti-facist and anti-racist groups in order to mobilise communities against organisations that stir up racial hatred.
- **Age UK** aims to improve later life for everyone through information and advice, services, campaigns, products, training and research.

- **The Fawcett Society** campaigns for **equality** between women and men in the UK on pay, pensions, poverty, **justice** and politics.
- **Stonewall** is an organisation that works for equality and justice for lesbians, gay men and bisexuals.

Key terms

Equality – where everyone has the same value and importance

Justice – treating people fairly

How religious people can respond to prejudice and the victims of it

Revised

- Pray.
- Look to holy books to help – see what they say.
- Individuals can speak to religious leaders.
- Campaign for change.
- Petition local councils and/or government.
- Education – through school assemblies.

Exam tip

These are standard answers that can be used in any topic where the question asks you 'What can religious people do to help …'. Just choose from the list any that apply to the topic you are asked about and make them relevant. For example:

- Pray *for those who suffer from prejudice* (this addresses the question!!).
- See what the holy book says *about homophobia* (this addresses the question!!).

Topic basics 4: Famous individuals

Martin Luther King Jr (1929–1968)

Revised

- Black Baptist minister in the USA in the 1950s and 1960s.
- Leader of the US civil rights movement.
- Used political speeches, sit-ins, marches, boycotts, etc. as a method of political pressure for change (all direct non-violent action).
- His actions were based on his Christian belief that God created us all equal.
- He was assassinated in 1968 but had gained many equal rights for blacks, and is now remembered in an annual holiday in the USA.

Successes – his legacy

- Equal rights, e.g. on bus transport.
- Segregation is now illegal in the USA.
- Equal civil rights – the vote for black Americans.
- Set the ball rolling for future black leaders such as Reverend Jesse Jackson.
- Barack Obama is MLK's greatest legacy, as his election proves America is open to people of all races as the country's leader.

Exam tip

Questions are usually about how the individual you choose to write about worked to fight against prejudice. Don't fall into the trap of simply giving a full life story!

Mohandas K. Gandhi (1869–1948)

Revised ☐

- In the 1890s Gandhi worked in South Africa for the rights of migrant Indian workers.
- Led a movement against the British Empire for Indian independence in the 1930s and 1940s.
- Used non-violent direct action in India, such as marches, boycotts and hunger strikes.
- Also campaigned against the caste system in India, setting examples.
- Gandhi was assassinated in 1948.

Successes – his legacy

- In 1914 the South African government accepted many of his demands for the Indian people, giving them greater rights.
- In 1947 British rule in India ended, and the country gained independence.
- People's attitudes began to change towards the caste system so that some groups within Hindu society completely accepted the 'Untouchables', and they came to have more rights under law.
- His non-violent values and methods have been used and drawn on by other campaigners (e.g. Martin Luther King Jr).

> **Common mistakes**
>
> Candidates often learn what the person does, but forget to learn why they do it – both are important.
>
> Revised ☐

Archbishop Desmond Tutu (1931–present day)

Revised ☐

- South African black archbishop.
- Fought against the apartheid system of segregation.
- Organised a non-violent struggle using marches, boycotts and petitions.
- Brought the issue of apartheid to worldwide attention, which helped to bring pressure on the government to end the system.

Successes so far

- Apartheid system dismantled.
- Elections held – first black president elected (Nelson Mandela).
- His work led to South Africa fielding international sports teams which included people of all races.
- Has shown that injustice can be fought successfully in a peaceful way.

> **Exam tip**
>
> Remember the face so that you get the facts right about the person you decide to revise!

Religious teachings on religion and prejudice: good teachings to learn

Revised

Sikhism

- 'Using the same mud, the creator has created many ways' (Guru Granth Sahib).
- Those who love God, love everyone.
- God created everyone so all are equal and deserve the same treatment and respect (Mool Mantra).
- The use of the Langar suggests everyone is welcome – Sikh or not.
- 'God is without caste' (Guru Gobind Singh).

Buddhism

- Five Precepts state 'do not harm others or use harmful language'.
- Metta (loving kindness) should be used by all.
- Everyone is equal and welcome in the sangha.
- Prejudice creates bad karma.
- Compassion should be the centre of all actions.

Christianity

- God created all of us equal.
- 'There is neither Jew nor Gentile, slave or free man, male or female. We are all one in Christ' (New Testament).
- Do to others as you would want others to do to you.
- Jesus said love your neighbour.
- In the story of the Good Samaritan, the man is helped because he needs it, not because of who he was or wasn't.

All religions teach:

- respect
- community
- tolerance
- justice
- fairness
- equality
- harmony

Judaism

- G-d created all of us equal.
- The Torah tells Jews to welcome and not persecute strangers.
- The Nevi'im states Jews should practise justice, love and kindness to all.
- Treat others as you wish to be treated.
- Jews should live in harmony with non-Jews.

Islam

- Difference was Allah's design so persecution is unjustified.
- Allah loves the fair minded.
- Muhammad (pbuh) allowed a black African man to do the call to prayer.
- The Muslim Declaration of Human Rights states all people are equal.
- On Hajj everyone is equal in dress and action.

Hinduism

- Belief in non-violence (ahimsa) and respect for all.
- Compassion is a key belief with the desire to improve things for others.
- Hurting others can lead to bad karma and rebirth.
- Everyone has an atman so all are equal.
- The Bhagavad Gita states that to reach liberation you should work for others.

Common mistakes

Many candidates just list teachings or beliefs, and let the examiner make sense of them for the question – it means they get lower marks. For example, if you say 'Christians believe in love your neighbour', you need to say why that is relevant to the question.

Revised

Exam tip

Candidates who use specific teachings make their answers clearer, and get better marks.

Exam tip

General teachings about prejudice can be used to answer any specific type of prejudice question.

What questions on this topic look like:
Religion and prejudice

Check back to pages 11–12 to see the grids examiners use to mark questions worth three or more marks.

This page contains a range of examples of questions that could be on an exam paper for this topic. Practise them all to strengthen your knowledge and technique while revising. Check the website for answers to some of these, with tips.

1   What is meant by racism?   [1]
2   What is meant by prejudice?   [1]
3   Name **one** organisation that fights against prejudice.   [1]
4   Explain what is meant by religious prejudice.   [2]
5   Give **two** reasons why some people are prejudiced.   [2]
6   Why might a religious believer disagree with discrimination?   [2]
7   Describe the work of an individual who has tried to end prejudice.   [3]
8   'Religious people should support the victims of prejudice.' What do you think? Explain your opinion.   [3]
9   'It is always wrong for religious people to be prejudiced.' What do you think? Explain your opinion.   [3]
10 Explain why religious believers think prejudice is wrong.   [4]
11 Explain religious attitudes to positive discrimination.   [4]
12 Explain how religious believers could work to reduce prejudice.   [4]
13 Explain religious attitudes to sexism. Refer to beliefs and teachings in your answer.   [5]
14 Explain, using beliefs and teachings, religious attitudes to ageism.   [5]
15 Explain why religious believers have tried to end prejudice.   [5]
16 'It is impossible to stop discrimination.' Do you agree? Give reasons and explain your answer, showing you have thought about more than one point of view. Refer to religious arguments in your answer.   [6]
17 'Racism is the worst form of prejudice.' Do you agree? Give reasons and explain your answer, showing you have thought about more than one point of view. Refer to religious arguments in your answer.   [6]
18 'It is never right to show prejudice.' Do you agree? Give reasons and explain your answer, showing you have thought about more than one point of view. Refer to religious arguments in your answer.   [6]

Online

Exam tip

Did you know that F-grade candidates usually only give very short answers to questions? They give one idea and move on to the next question – whatever mark is available. If this is you, force yourself to give two answers every time. You will increase your marks (and that means your grade).

Did you know that C-grade candidates often only give a couple of ideas for each answer? They can give a range of ideas, and sometimes they explain those ideas, but don't do it consistently across all their answers. If this is you, make yourself stop and think when you make a point – always explain.

Did you know that A-grade candidates usually write in paragraphs, which means they automatically explain what they say?

So, which one are you?

Topic 4 Religion and early life

Key knowledge

- When life begins.
- Children as a **blessing** and the **miracle of life**.
- What we mean by abortion.
- Why women have abortions.
- Arguments around the quality or **sanctity of life**.
- Abortion Law.
- Religious attitudes to abortion.
- The rights of all those involved – mother, father, foetus.
- Alternatives to abortion.
- The work of pressure groups.

Key terms

Blessing – the baby can be seen as a gift from God to the parents

Miracle of life – the idea that the pregnancy process is so special, it's a miracle

Sanctity of life – life is special and sacred, often considered as such because it is life from God

Topic basics 1: About children

When does life begin?

Revised ☐

Different ideas have been put forward for when life begins. They include:

- at **conception** when the sperm meets the egg
- when the backbone begins to develop – there is a clear shape
- when the foetus has a heart
- at birth when life is independent of the mother's body and can survive on its own.

Key term

Conception – when the sperm meets the egg to fertilise it, after which point a pregnancy has begun

Why some people want children

Revised ☐

- To carry on the family name and religion.
- It fulfils marriage promises and 'completes' the family.
- The child is the expression of the love that the couple share.
- Religious duty to accept this gift of life from God.

Why some people don't have children

Revised ☐

- Too expensive.
- Not ready for the responsibility.
- Not in a stable or happy relationship.
- Too young or old, or not in a position to care for a child.
- Medical reasons that prevent them from having a child, or mean they won't risk having a child.

Exam tip

There are key things to think about that underpin this topic:

- How sacred and valuable life is.
- The value of the life of the mother over the foetus.
- Whether you can kill something that has not been born.
- Whether there are any acceptable reasons for abortion.

Have opinions on all those – you will need them in the exam.

The Law

Before 1967, **abortion** was totally illegal yet it still happened. There were around 100,000 cases a year and many women died as it was being carried out by unregistered people. Women were desperate and risked their lives to 'get rid' of the foetus. So regulation was required:

The 1967 Abortion Act

The **1967 Abortion Act** states that abortion is illegal in Britain, but:

- It can be carried out in specific circumstances where two doctors agree:
  - there is danger to the woman's mental or physical health
  - that the foetus will be born with physical or mental disabilities
  - that the welfare of existing children may be affected.
- The limit for an abortion to take place was 28 weeks.
- It must be done by a registered doctor in a registered hospital or clinic.

The Human Fertilisation and Embryology Act 1990

Although this law is **mainly about fertility treatments and embryo research**, it also **amended the 1967 Act**. The limit was **reduced to 24 weeks**, because of **advances in medical knowledge** about gestation and medical science. In reality the majority of abortions take place within the **first 12 weeks** of pregnancy anyway.

These Acts **opened abortion up to any woman** who wanted one as it is difficult to think of any situation a woman might find herself in that **would not fit** into any of the three clauses. As a result, there has been a **massive increase** in numbers of abortions and there is still **great debate** as to the rights and wrongs of it.

> **Key terms**
>
> **Abortion** – deliberate expulsion of the foetus from the womb, with the intention for it to never become a living person
>
> **1967 Abortion Act** – the UK law on abortion limit of 28 weeks with conditions
>
> **Human Fertilisation and Embryology Act 1990** – the law that reduced the abortion limit to 24 weeks

> **Exam tip**
>
> Key information is in bold here to aid your revision.

Topic basics 2: Arguments for and against abortion

The rights of the foetus (Pro-life)

Pro-life arguments are totally against abortion, and include the following ideas:

- The life of the foetus is at least as important and for some more important than the life of the mother.
- The foetus must have someone speaking for it (an advocate).
- All life has potential and should be given the chance.
- Abortion is murder – murder is wrong.
- All life is sacred and must be protected.
- God created all life so humans must protect it.
- A foetus should never be discarded as waste.
- We must not abort for a disability as we should not judge the **quality of life** of another.

> **Exam tip**
>
> You should learn three or four reasons for and against abortion in preparation for the exam.

> **Key terms**
>
> **Pro-life** – arguments focusing on the rights of the foetus to have life
>
> **Quality of life** – what a person's life should be like for it to be worth living

Prolife.org.uk

This organisation was set up to **secure the rights of all to life**, and its work is related to any issue of life – abortion, suicide and euthanasia. They believe in **educating people** that the right to life is the **basic human right**. They **campaign politically** for changes in the law, e.g. to make abortion completely illegal. A big part of their work is to keep the issues **high profile** in the media so that people have to think about it, and will help them change the law.

Exam tip

Key information is in bold here to aid your revision.

Exam tip

You might be asked to briefly describe the work of a pressure group or organisation that works for the rights of the unborn child, or for the right to choose. Learn these examples. You can also refer to them in other questions on abortion.

The woman's right to choose (pro-choice)

Revised

Pro-choice arguments defend the woman's rights to choose, and her right to decide what happens to her body, including abortion. They are not defending abortion, taking the view it is a necessary evil. The arguments are focused on the woman not the foetus, and include the following:

Key term

Pro-choice – arguments focusing on the mother's right to choose

- A woman has the right to decide what happens to her body.
- Some foetuses are so damaged it would be cruel to let them be born.
- If the woman's life is at risk she should have the right to abortion.
- Where rape has occurred then abortion has to be available as an option.
- The foetus cannot survive outside the womb until a certain point, so it is not a life in its own right until that point.
- Women would have abortions anyway, just not safe ones.

Abortion rights (the National Pro-Choice campaign)

The organisation was set up to **secure the rights of women** to have abortions. They believe that a woman is the **best one to decide** whether to carry on with her pregnancy. They campaign **against restrictions in the law**, and **for better provision** and women friendly NHS funded abortion services. They want to **stop doctors from blocking** abortion requests. They use **petitions, public meetings and publications** to get their message across, as well as political campaigning.

Exam tip

Key information in bold here to aid your revision.

Topic basics 3: Religious attitudes to abortion

Religious attitudes to abortion

Revised

Buddhism	Buddhist texts do not mention abortion. However, Buddhism believes that taking life is wrong and that life begins at conception. Abortion is seen as violent, gives the foetus no rights and does not show compassion. Also bad karma may be created for the doctor or mother because of the intention to harm a living being. Having said that, at times abortion can lead to less suffering and so Buddhists accept it on these few occasions.
Christianity	Christians believe that only God has the right to take life; after all he created it. The Roman Catholic Church is totally against abortion and teaches that life must be protected. Many Protestants accept abortion as a necessary evil but stress it must be as a last resort and after much careful thought.

Hinduism ॐ	In the main, Hindus believe that abortion is wrong. However, it is common in India for social and cultural reasons (poverty and the need for male children). Abortion is believed to bring bad karma and prevent the foetus' soul from working through a lifetime. Some scriptures say those who abort will be aborted many times themselves. However, it is accepted in the case of saving the mother's life.
Islam ☪	Muslims believe abortion is wrong but Shari'ah law does allow it as a necessary evil. Having an abortion destroys Allah's plan for a life. It is believed that the soul enters the foetus at 40 or 120 days, therefore before these times abortion is allowed (but not seen as abortion as the foetus is just blood and cells). It is usually acceptable where the woman's life is at risk, because her duty to her existing family is seen as more important.
Judaism ♁	Jewish views vary according to the type of Judaism they follow. Most Jewish people accept abortion for medical reasons, for example a woman's life takes priority if it is in danger, because the foetus is part of the woman not a life in itself. Some Rabbis allow for the woman's mental state here as well, for example in the case of rape. In cases of severe deformity, abortion can be considered.
Sikhism ☬	There are no direct teachings about abortion in Sikhism, so it is up to individuals to make this decision. For most Sikhs, abortion is seen as morally wrong as life starts at conception, and so it is a form of murder as the intention is to destroy life. Abortion also goes against the idea of not harming others and sewa (service to others). It is also seen as interfering with God's creation.

Exam tip

These are general attitudes. Learn them to get the idea of how religions feel about abortion, but learn specific teachings to go with them.

Topic basics 4: Quality of life and the question of rights

Quality of life argument
Revised ☐

'Quality of life' means what someone's life is like – how good it is, how easy it is for the person to live an ordinary life. It is an argument sometimes used to support abortion. This is mainly true of abortion on the grounds of disability, because the argument is that the *disability affects the quality of life* of the person when born, and this is unfair, for example a foetus that has been diagnosed as having a severe physical or mental disability, or a foetus that will never as a person be able to look after themselves.

Always true?

However, this means *other people making judgements* about whether a life is worth living, because the foetus has no say, nor even a chance to experience life and be able to make the decision as to whether it is worth living or not.

Having said that, as a percentage of the number of abortions carried out, it is *rare to see an abortion requested because of disability* arguments. The people making the decisions are not trying to be cruel, rather they are trying to be compassionate to the foetus. The action is seen as a *necessary evil* – the kindest thing to do.

Quality of life of the existing family

The argument about quality of life also considers whether it is right for this family to have this child. Perhaps they have many children already and are struggling to look after them; perhaps they have a severely disabled child already who needs so much care they could not look after another. In each of these cases, people who disagree with abortion would see the foetus as innocent, and would suggest other options.

> **Exam tip**
>
> Make sure you can define 'quality of life', and know at least one example of abortion for the reason of 'quality of life'. Questions on this aspect often confuse candidates but there is no need, if you have practised ahead of time.

Questions focused on quality of life

Revised ☐

If faced with a question about quality of life, use these ideas for your written argument: what if the foetus was blind and deaf, totally paralysed, had severe mental disability, and would need 24-hour care and many operations? In these cases we could say the abortion was the right choice because:

- it prevented suffering and/or early painful death
- the person would have no independence
- the person would not be able to enjoy life to the full
- the person would potentially be the victim of discrimination.

But:

- Have we the right to decide the quality of life of another?
- Many disabled people are able to enjoy and achieve in life.
- Do you miss what you never had, e.g. sight or hearing?
- Life should always be given a chance and medical science could help in the future.

You could also make the point that not all disabilities are so bad, and the system could be abused because, for example, a woman doesn't want a child with a cleft palate.

> **Common mistakes**
>
> Candidates often mix up 'quality of life' and 'sanctity of life'. If you get them wrong in the exam, you lose marks. Quality means how good – don't forget.
>
> Revised ☐

Whose right is it to choose?

Revised ☐

This is often used as an evaluation question because it allows many agree and disagree answers. You could explore the following:

- woman
- husband
- boyfriend
- parents
- religious leader
- doctor.

The circumstances the woman finds herself in make a difference to your answer, for example if she is living in very poor circumstances, or already has a child with a disability. So does when and how the child was conceived, for example, if she was too young, or if she was raped.

> **Exam tip**
>
> Candidates who make themselves start thinking using the phrase 'It depends …' often have better answers, because they are already broadening the potential for answers. Consider 'The father should have equal rights in deciding on an abortion'. Well, it depends whether he knows or not … it depends if she is going to die … You get the idea.

You need to be able to have ideas for and against for the people in the list and think: 'What if ... the woman was young, not married, still at school, religious, has health problems', etc.

There is often no right or wrong answer here; as long as your ideas are sensible and logical you will get marks.

Common mistakes

Often 'whose right to decide' is asked in an evaluative question, and candidates just write about abortion being right or wrong. 'Rights' is about who should get to decide about having the abortion – should it be the mother, the father, or anyone else, and should each person carry equal weight in the decision – so answer the right question!

Revised ☐

Alternatives to abortion
Revised ☐

The exam could ask you what other options are available to the woman. You need to think about the pros and cons of the alternatives.

- Complete the pregnancy, and keep the child: all could work out well, or the mother could face severe problems looking after, loving or providing for the child.

- Choose to risk own life: both might survive. Or in the case of an ectopic pregnancy or cancer, for example, the mother might die leaving the child alone or be seriously ill for life.

- **Fostering**: this gives the chance for the child to be looked after by its natural mother some time later. The child may be confused and feel given up on and unwanted. The foster family may not work out.

- **Adoption**: the child is brought up by a good family but may want to find the real parents and may face problems of feeling unwanted.

These are just some suggestions to get you thinking. Remember there are no right or wrong decisions. Try to be open-minded and accept that there are different points of view. This position leads to much better answers.

Key terms

Fostering – to temporarily look after a child that is not your own. It is still legally its mother's

Adoption – to take legal responsibility for a child that is not your own

Exam tip

Be careful not to be blinded by your own strong beliefs about this topic. This leads to poor unbalanced answers.

Religious teachings on religion and early life: good teachings to learn

Sikhism

- Life begins at conception.
- All life is special and should be respected.
- God fills us with light so we can be born.
- God created us, gave us life and will take it away.
- Sikhs should not harm others.

Buddhism

- The First Precept guides us to help, not harm, others and reduce suffering.
- Metta (compassion) – loving kindness should be used by all.
- Life is special and to be protected.
- Intention is all important, e.g. the reasons for abortion.
- Life begins at conception.

Christianity

- God gives life and takes it away – not us (Old Testament).
- All life is sacred – special to God.
- All humans are created in the image of God (Genesis).
- God planned all our lives.
- The Ten Commandments say 'Do not kill'.

All religions teach:
- rights
- sanctity of life
- miracle of life
- quality of life

Judaism

- The foetus is as special as all life.
- Abortion under Jewish law is not murder.
- Emphasis is on life and new life, not the destruction of it.
- We only gain full human status when we have been born.
- Until the fortieth day the foetus is 'mere water'.

Islam

- Life is sacred (Qur'an).
- Allah decides the time of our birth and death, and has planned our lives.
- We are all created from a clot of blood and known by Allah (Qur'an).
- It is wrong to kill.
- Ensoulment (when the soul becomes part of the foetus) is after 40 days, not at conception.

Hinduism

- Belief in non-violence (ahimsa) and respect for all.
- Life is sacred.
- A woman who aborts her child loses her caste and karma is affected.
- Abortion is as bad as killing a priest or parents.
- Abortionists are among the worst of sinners.

Exam tip

Remember you only need to look at the religion(s) you have been taught.

Remember to APPLY the teaching to the question after you have stated it – see how simple this is by referring to page 9.

For most answers probably three specific teachings plus the generic ones will be sufficient.

What questions on this topic look like:
Religion and early life

Check back to pages 11–12 to see the grids examiners use to mark questions worth three or more marks.

This page contains a range of examples of questions that could be on an exam paper for this topic. Practise them all to strengthen your knowledge and technique while revising.

1 What is meant by abortion? [1]

2 What is meant by pro-choice? [1]

3 Explain what is meant by sanctity of life. [2]

4 Give **two** reasons why some women choose to have an abortion. [2]

5 Give **two** reasons why some couples choose to have children. [2]

6 Explain ideas about when life begins. [3]

7 Describe what the law says about abortion. [3]

8 'Religious people should not have abortions.' What do you think? Explain your opinion. [3]

9 Explain why some religious believers might believe children to be a blessing on a marriage. [4]

10 Explain religious attitudes to having children. Refer to beliefs and teachings in your answer. [4]

11 Explain the circumstances that might lead a person to consider abortion. [4]

12 Explain why some religious believers disagree with abortion. Use beliefs and teachings in your answer. [5]

13 Using examples, explain why religious believers might agree with abortion. Use beliefs and teachings in your answer. [5]

14 Explain how the concepts of sanctity of life and quality of life can affect a person's decision regarding abortion. [5]

15 'All life begins at conception.' Do you agree? Give reasons for your answer, showing you have thought about more than one point of view. Refer to religious arguments in your answer. [6]

16 'Abortion should only be available if a woman's life is in danger.' Do you agree? Give reasons for your answer, showing you have thought about more than one point of view. Refer to religious arguments in your answer. [6]

17 'The father should have the right to stop a woman having an abortion.' Do you agree? Give reasons for your answer, showing you have thought about more than one point of view. Refer to religious arguments in your answer. [6]

Online

Topic 5 Religion, war and peace

- The concepts of peace, justice and the sanctity of life.
- The causes of war.
- 'Just War' and 'Holy War'.
- Religious attitudes to:
  - pacifism
  - war
  - helping victims of war
  - nuclear war
  - terrorism.
- The work of organisations that help the victims of war.
- The work of a religious believer who has worked for peace.
- The role of peacekeeping forces such as the United Nations and NATO.

Topic basics 1: Key concepts about war

Key concepts ──────────────────────────────── Revised ☐

Learn these terms and apply them when asked about religious attitudes.

Peace

Peace is a virtue in all religions and means:

- absence of **war**
- harmony between people and nations
- justice for all.

Justice

Justice is:

- what is right and fair
- respect for freedom
- just laws and punishment for offenders
- protection of individual and group rights.

Sanctity of life

Sanctity of life refers to the idea that life is:

- a gift of God
- sacred and holy
- valuable and precious
- purposeful.

Key terms

Peace – the absence of war or conflict between groups or nations

War – two or more sides or nations involved in armed conflict

Justice – to bring about what is right and fair for all people, correcting wrongs

Sanctity of life – the belief that life is special and sacred

Exam tip

The key concepts can be used to develop your answers to show why religious believers hold the attitudes they do. For example, many religious believers are pacifists because they believe in the sanctity of life.

Types of war

- Between nations, e.g. the First and Second World Wars, Vietnam War, Falklands War, Gulf War.
- Civil wars, e.g. former Yugoslavia, Sierra Leone, Rwanda.
- War against **terrorism**, e.g. Allies against Al Qaeda in specific countries such as Pakistan, and around the world.

Causes of war

- Defence against invader.
- Defence of religion, freedoms, way of life.
- Defence of a weaker nation.
- Pre-emptive strike to prevent expected attack.
- To gain land or resources.
- To remove an unjust leader.
- To end injustice such as genocide (the wholesale murder of an ethnic group within a country, by another ethnic group).

How are wars fought?

- Conventional – using military personal and regular weapons.
- **Weapons of mass destruction** – nuclear, biological, chemical, radiological.

Effects of war

- **Victims of war** – killed, maimed, orphaned, **refugees**.
- Soldiers – killed, traumatised, desensitised.
- Environment – destruction of landscape, hazardous areas, e.g. landmines.
- Economy – loss of farming and industry, cost of rebuild.
- Political – bitter tensions created between opposing forces that lead to future conflicts.

> **Key terms**
>
> **Terrorism** – the use of threats and violence by groups to create a climate of fear to achieve their aims
>
> **Weapons of mass destruction (WMDs)** – weapons that can kill large numbers of people and destroy vast areas of land
>
> **Victims of war** – civilians who are affected by war
>
> **Refugees** – people who are forced to leave their homes to find safety elsewhere

> **Exam tip**
>
> No religious tradition supports the use of WMDs because they go against the sanctity of life, justice and do not fit the Just War theory. However, some believers may support the view that these weapons are retained, but only as a deterrent.

Topic basics 2: Just War and Holy War

Just War theory

Revised

The **Just War** theory is the religious criteria (rules) for engaging in war. It is called a 'Just' war because it comes from the belief that sometimes a war needs to be fought to achieve justice, especially where innocent people are being persecuted. Religious believers in Christianity and Sikhism should only participate in fighting a war if it fits with all the following rules.

- Controlled by a just authority, e.g. an elected government, a religious leader.
- Just cause, e.g. it must be to achieve justice, not for gain or revenge.
- Aim is clear, e.g. to promote good over evil, an objective that when met brings the war to an end.

> **Key term**
>
> **Just War** – the rules of war which permit a religious person to fight, found in Christian and Sikh teachings

> **Exam tip**
>
> The CLOPJAW acrostic will help you remember these seven criteria of a Just War (see page 121).

- Last resort – all diplomatic methods tried first such as negotiation, peace talks.
- Winnable – the objective must be achievable; it is wrong to risk life if war cannot be won.
- Proportional – the method of fighting must be fair, no excessive use of weaponry, civilians protected.
- Good outcome – the benefits of the war outweigh the evil of war.

Common mistakes   Revised

- Proportional does not mean equal weapons, it means reasonable force to achieve the objective.
- When asked to explain the Just War theory many candidates simply list the points. This gets a very low mark even if several of the points are recalled. To explain means to include a development of the point made.

Holy War   Revised

In Islam a **Holy War** is the same as the Christian Just War. Believers have to fight because it is a religious duty. It is considered 'Holy' because it is sanctioned by Allah (God). The war must be fought keeping the following rules:

- Fought for God or faith.
- Last resort – the enemy must have an opportunity to make peace.
- Believers obligated to fight.
- Conducted fairly – just treatment of the enemy.
- Protection of civilians and the landscape; certain buildings such as hospitals and holy buildings should be protected, and densely populated civilian areas should not be targeted.
- Justice and peace should be restored at the end of the war.
- The war must end when the aim has been achieved.

Key term

Holy War – fighting for a religious cause or God, found in Christian and Islamic teachings

Religious attitudes to Just and Holy Wars   Revised

Religions have different attitudes to war and you will need to be sure you know what the specific views are of the religion(s) you are studying. If a war fulfils the criteria here, many believers will be prepared to support and even fight in the war. Some believers see no distinction between a Just War and a Holy War and will say that a war fought for justice is fighting for God. Some believers, however, will say war is always wrong and refuse to fight.

Topic basics 3: War in the modern world

Weapons of mass destruction (WMDs) are modern weapons that can kill many people and cause immense destruction to the environment. They include biological, chemical and nuclear weapons.

The nuclear debate: Should countries have nuclear weapons?

Revised

Reasons for proliferation (increase in number of countries with nuclear weapons)

- Nuclear weapons are seen as a deterrent which discourage attack and maintain peace – they would never be used because of 'mutually assured destruction' (MAD): if two countries used nuclear weapons against each other, both would get destroyed.
- Countries that don't have nuclear weapons feel they should be allowed to have them to defend themselves against those that do.
- Countries that are allies in war share military technology, including nuclear weapons.
- There are huge risks and expense involved in destroying these weapons, which puts countries off destroying them.

Reasons for disarmament (removal of nuclear weapons)

- **Nuclear proliferation** makes the use of nuclear weapons more likely.
- No moral justification for their use, because their effect is indiscriminate, affecting civilians, land and buildings over many miles and for many years.
- Waste of valuable resources to produce them which could be used more effectively.
- Monetary cost of these weapons for their production and storage could be used for peaceful means and the benefit of mankind, such as reducing poverty.
- The threat of nuclear weapons makes more countries develop them to defend themselves.

> **Exam tip**
>
> When evaluating this topic you might find that you only have religious arguments for the removal of nuclear weapons. It is perfectly acceptable in six-mark responses to have only religious arguments in one half of your answer. As long as you show that there is an alternative viewpoint (which does not necessarily have to be a religious one) you can still achieve maximum marks.

> **Key term**
>
> **Nuclear proliferation** – the increase in the number of countries that have nuclear weapons

Religious attitudes to WMDs

Revised

- Use of WMDs, including nuclear weapons, is wrong; their effects are extreme and uncontrollable.
- WMDs are against Just War and Holy War rules; they destroy God's creation.
- WMDs are against the religious principles of peace, justice and sanctity of life.

- WMDs are used as a means of oppression – chemical weapons have been used by governments against their own people, e.g. in Iraq and Syria; they are wrong.
- Some believers accept the maintaining of nuclear weapons as a deterrent, but they should never be used.

What is terrorism?

Revised

- Use of violence to create fear.
- Indiscriminate targeting of civilians and civilian areas.
- Non-democratic.
- Used to promote minority views, often fundamentalist.

Religious attitudes to terrorism

Revised

- Terrorism is against the principles of religious beliefs; it ignores justice and leads to indiscriminate killing and harm.
- Religious teachings promote peace, justice and respect for life.
- A minority of fundamentalists use terrorist tactics; they are condemned by the majority of other religious believers.

Topic basics 4: Responses to war and peace

The impacts of war can leave people in desperate situations. The immediate effects of loss of life, wounding of soldiers and civilians, homelessness and the destruction of the environment create many problems. Charities and the international community have to act to reduce the impact of war on the victims and to help to try to alleviate suffering and establish peace so that it does not happen again.

Responses to war

Revised

Support for victims of war

You need to know about organisations that help the victims of war. These can include civilian casualties and refugees as well as the soldiers and families of those who fight in the war. These organisations are often charities, but can include government supported services such as the armed forces, hospitals and paramedics. After all, they too help people caught in conflicts.

Charities that work for the victims of war include: the Red Cross, Red Crescent, Médecins Sans Frontières, Help for Heroes and the Poppy Appeal. They help the victims of war by providing both short-term aid (immediate help) and long-term aid (on-going long-term support).

The work of these organisations includes:

- providing humanitarian aid, e.g. food, medical care, shelter, protection from attack
- counselling and support for those who have lost loved ones to conflict, been abused during conflict, permanently maimed
- support when conflict ends, e.g. rebuilding, locating lost family, care of orphans
- campaigns to bring an end to war and conflict.

Peacekeeping forces

Peacekeeping forces are organisations that work to create world peace. They are different to charities because the aim of these groups is to promote harmony and co-operation between countries. They aim to promote international law and security, economic and social progress. They try to do this through dialogue and the creation of international treaties (agreements between countries). They include the United Nations (UN) and NATO. Peacekeeping work includes:

- protection of human rights in conflict zones
- use of international pressure such as sanctions to end human rights abuses
- use of military forces to implement peace agreements, monitor elections, conduct disarmament, etc.
- brokering of peace agreements through diplomacy
- supporting allied nations threatened by others.

Key term

Peacekeeping forces – organisations that work in areas of conflict to protect victims of war and establish and maintain peace between groups and nations

Common mistakes

Candidates sometimes confuse the work of supporting the victims of war with the work of peacekeeping forces. These are two very different types of organisation and work. Make sure that if you are asked about a peacekeeping organisation you focus on the work they do to promote peace, not humanitarian aid.

Revised

Peace

Peace is the absence of war and the presence of harmony between countries and communities.

Religious views

- Promoted by all religious faiths.
- The Golden Rule, e.g. treat people how you wish to be treated is found in all religious traditions.
- Necessary for people's physical and spiritual well-being.
- Some religious believers are pacifists.

Pacifism

People who believe in **pacifism** include Quakers, Buddhists, the Dalai Lama and Martin Luther King Jr. Pacifists:

- oppose all use of war and violent conflict
- believe in the sanctity of life
- believe peace can be achieved using non-violent methods
- are often conscientious objectors who refuse to participate directly in fighting wars on moral grounds.

Exam tip

The best answers to questions about peace make use of religious teachings that are about peace specifically, not just about war.

Key term

Pacifism – the belief that all violence is wrong

Individuals working for peace

Mohandas K. Gandhi (1869–1948)

- Hindu leader of India who campaigned for Indian independence from British rule in the 1930s and 1940s.
- Campaigned against apartheid and the Pass laws in South Africa.
- Emphasised need for ahimsa (non-violence).
- Developed the principle of satyagraha – resistance to oppression through non-violence.
- Led an organised programme of civil disobedience to achieve aims, e.g. the Salt March.

Dalai Lama (1935–present day)

- Spiritual leader of Tibetan Buddhists.
- Campaigns for Tibetan liberation from Chinese rule.
- Forced into exile from Tibet by the Chinese government.
- Has promoted the preservation of Tibetan culture by refugees in India.
- Believes all violence is wrong, that peace is found in mutual respect.
- Has become an international symbol of peace.

Dietrich Bonhoeffer (1906–1945)

- Christian theologian and pacifist who founded the Confessing Church in Nazi-ruled Germany.
- Spoke out against Nazi human rights abuses.
- Believed principles must be placed aside to overcome evil, even if this leads to personal suffering.
- Helped Jews escape from death camps and worked to overthrow the Nazi Party.
- Was executed for his part in a plot to assassinate Hitler.

Exam tip

If asked about the work of a religious believer who has campaigned for peace, ensure your response focuses on what they did rather than who they were.

Common mistakes

Some candidates write about campaigners like Nelson Mandela who were not religious leaders. Do not use them as examples if asked to write about the work of a religious believer who has campaigned for peace.

Religious teachings on religion, war and peace: good teachings to learn

Sikhism

- 'As you value yourself, so value others, cause suffering to no one' (Guru Granth Sahib).
- 'When all else fails, it is right to draw the sword' (Guru Gobind Singh).
- 'His followers were to emerge as splendid warriors … having taken the baptism of the sword, would thence forward be firmly attached to the sword' (Guru Granth Sahib).
- 'The Lord is a haven of peace' (Adi Granth).
- 'Those who serve God find peace' (Guru Ram Das).

Buddhism

- The First Moral Precept teaches not to harm others.
- 'Those who are free of resentful thoughts surely find peace' (Buddha).
- 'Hatred does not cease by hatred, hatred ceases by love' (Dhammapada).
- 'He should not kill a living being, nor cause it to be killed, nor should he incite another to kill' (Dhammapada).
- 'Peace can exist if everyone respects all others' (Dalai Lama).

Christianity

- 'Those who live by the sword die by the sword' (Jesus).
- 'Blessed are the peacemakers, for they shall be called the children of God' (Jesus in The Beatitudes).
- 'Love your neighbour' (Jesus).
- 'If someone slaps you on the right cheek, turn to him the other' (Jesus).
- 'Everyone must commit themselves to peace' (Pope John Paul II).

All religions teach:
- peace
- justice
- sanctity of life

Judaism

- 'What is harmful to yourself, do not do to fellow man' (Rabbi Hillel).
- 'Get ready for war, call out your best warriors. Let your fighting men advance for the attack' (Ketuvim).
- 'It shall come to pass … nation shall not lift up sword against nation, neither shall they learn war anymore' (Nevi'im).
- 'If they refuse to make peace and they engage you in battle, lay siege to that city' (Torah).
- 'By three things is the world preserved, on justice, on truth and on peace' (Rabbi Hillel).

Islam

- 'Fight in the cause of Allah those who fight you, but do not transgress limits … if they cease let there be no hostility' (Qur'an).
- Lesser Jihad – to fight in the name of Allah and defend one's faith.
- 'Hate your enemy mildly, for he may become your friend one day' (Hadith).
- 'Fight them until there is no more oppression and there justice prevails' (Qur'an).
- 'Allah loves those who fight in His cause' (Qur'an).

Hinduism

- 'I object to violence because the good it appears to do is only temporary, the evil is permanent' (Gandhi).
- 'The pursuit of truth does not permit violence being inflicted on one's opponent' (Gandhi).
- Ahimsa – the Hindu principle of non-violence to all living things.
- 'This is the sum of duty, do nothing to others which if done to you could cause pain' (Mahabharata).
- 'If you do not fight in this just war, you will neglect your duty, harm your reputation and commit the sin of omission' (Bhagavad Gita).

Exam tip

It is easy to forget to learn teachings (or anything else) about peace – make sure you learn teachings to use in the exam.

What questions on this topic look like:
Religion, war and peace

Check back to pages 11–12 to see the grids examiners use to mark questions worth three or more marks.

This page contains a range of examples of questions that could be on an exam paper for this topic. Practise them all to strengthen your knowledge and technique while revising. Check the website for answers to some of these, with tips.

1   What is a pacifist?   [1]
2   What is terrorism?   [1]
3   Give **two** reasons why some countries go to war.   [2]
4   Give **two** ways that people are affected by war.   [2]
5   Explain what is meant by weapons of mass destruction.   [2]
6   Describe the work of **one** individual who has worked for peace.   [3]
7   Explain why many religious believers disagree with war.   [3]
8   'Religious believers should be pacifists.' What do you think? Explain your opinion.   [3]
9   Explain why some religious believers would not fight in a war.   [4]
10 Describe the work of one organisation that helps the victims of war.   [4]
11 Explain **two** reasons why many religious believers disagree with nuclear weapons.   [4]
12 Explain religious teachings about holy war.   [5]
13 Explain, using beliefs and teachings, religious attitudes to peace.   [5]
14 Explain religious attitudes to the use of peacekeeping forces.   [5]
15 'Religious people should never take part in terrorist acts.' Do you agree? Give reasons for your answer, showing you have thought about more than one point of view. Refer to religious arguments in your answer.   [6]
16 'Religious people should never take part in war.' Do you agree? Give reasons for your answer, showing you have thought about more than one point of view. Refer to religious arguments in your answer.   [6]
17 'Peace is impossible in the world.' Do you agree? Give reasons for your answer, showing you have thought about more than one point of view. Refer to religious arguments in your answer.   [6]

Online

Exam tip

Did you know an F-grade candidate will make barely any reference to religious teachings and beliefs and their answers will be of a superficial and general nature? If this is you, learn the teachings as you study.

Did you know a C-grade candidate will include some teachings and beliefs in their answers, but these will mostly be general ideas that have been paraphrased and sometimes will not really fit the topic they are discussing? If this is you, learn the specific ones from page 54.

Did you know an A-grade candidate will make very good use of teachings and beliefs. They will use specific references that exactly fit the topic they are discussing and paraphrases will be precise.

So, which one are you?

Topic 6 Religion and young people

Key knowledge

- Birth and **initiation ceremonies** in one religious tradition.
- The role of the home, upbringing, spirituality, moral codes and religious beliefs as an influence on decision making and life choices.
- Activities organised by faith groups for young people, their purpose and contribution.
- Commitment and membership of faith groups.
- Rights and responsibilities of young people including freedom of choice, relationships and rules.
- Problems and benefits for young people of commitment to faith.
- Role of schools including Religious Studies, assemblies and faith schools.

Key term

Initiation ceremonies – religious rituals performed to formally enter a person into a faith

Exam tip

For each of these areas you need to be able to explain specific terms, give examples to show you understand them, write accounts of ceremonies and explain symbols within them, understand why these ceremonies are performed and explain why people agree and disagree with the issues they raise.

Topic basics 1: Birth ceremonies

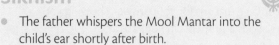 **Birth ceremonies in each religion** 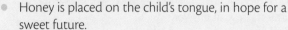 Revised

Sikhism

- The father whispers the Mool Mantar into the child's ear shortly after birth.
- Honey is placed on the child's tongue, in hope for a sweet future.
- The naming ceremony takes place in the gurdwara soon after birth.
  - The parents present ingredients for Karah Parshad and Romalla covers as gifts.
  - Readings are made from the Guru Granth Sahib.
  - The granthi stirs amrit (sugar water) with a kirpan (knife), and then drops of amrit are placed on the child's tongue; prayers are said for long life and sweet nature.
  - The granthi then opens the Guru Granth Sahib at a random page, and the first letter of the first word on the left-hand page becomes the initial for the child's name.
  - The parents choose a name, and the Granthi announces this to the congregation.
  - Karah Parshad is shared by the congregation and the parents make a donation to charity.

Judaism

- There are different ceremonies for boys and girls.
  - Male children are circumcised eight days after birth, even on a Sabbath.
  - A trained Mohel carries out the procedure, while the child is held by an honoured guest called a sandek.
  - The father reads a blessing from the Torah.
  - The mohel blesses the child and announces his name.
  - The mother feeds the child and celebrations are held.
- Female children have their name announced in synagogue at first Sabbath after the birth.
- Some Jews have a Zeved Habit ceremony for girls.
  - The Rabbi blesses the child in the home.
  - Celebrations follow.

Christianity

- Infant baptism is part of many Christian denominations – a ceremony entering the child into the Christian faith.
- The baby is dressed in white to symbolise purity.
- The priest asks the parents and godparents three questions.
- Water is taken from the font and sprinkled onto the baby's forehead three times.
- The priest says, 'In the name of the father, son and holy spirit', makes the symbol of the cross and announces the child's name.
- A lighted candle is given to the parents as symbol of Jesus' light in the world.

Buddhism

- There are no specific religious ceremonies, but there are cultural ones.
- A monk may visit the home to bless the child by chanting scriptures.
- Gifts are given to the sangha by the child's parents.
- The parents may also visit the temple and make offerings.
- Some Buddhists have the child named at a temple.
- Water is sprinkled on the child, symbolising cleanliness.

Hinduism

- Hindu ceremonies are called samskaras.
- Some take place before birth. There are two soon after birth, first of which is the Jatakarma:
  - The father makes the Om symbol on the baby's tongue with mixture of ghee and honey, which symbolises hope for child to have sweet nature.
  - The father also whispers the name of the Ultimate Reality into baby's ear to welcome him or her into the faith.
- Namakarana takes place ten to twelve days after birth:
  - The baby is dressed in new clothes and taken to the temple.
  - An astrologer reads out the child's horoscope, and the child's name is announced.
  - The family make a havan (fire sacrifice) and make offerings to deities.

Islam

- The tahneek ceremony takes place soon after birth.
  - The father whispers the Adhan (call to prayer) in child's right ear, and the Iqamah (call to prayer before salat) into the left ear.
  - The child is now welcomed into faith.
  - A date is placed on the child's tongue, symbolising hope for a sweet nature.
- The aqiqah ceremony takes place shortly afterwards.
  - The child's head is shaved, the hair weighed and the family make an equivalent donation of money – to purify the child.
  - Verses from Qur'an are read aloud.
  - The child's name is announced and Adhan is again whispered into the child's ear.
  - Male children are circumcised.
  - The family pay for an animal to be sacrificed and its meat given to poor.

Common mistakes

Birth ceremonies are connected with infants and so it does not make sense when evaluating to say that the baby should make their own choice. What you need to do is focus on evaluating whether the tradition is important to maintain.

Revised

Key term

Birth ceremonies – religious rituals that are performed when a child is born or in early infancy

Exam tip

Make sure that when asked to explain a ceremony you focus on the symbols that are used and say what they mean.

Topic basics 2: Ceremonies of commitment

Ceremonies of commitment

Buddhism

- There is no specific ceremony to become a Buddhist.
- Some choose to recite the Three Refuges to mark acceptance of the Buddhist way of life.
- Theravada Buddhists have a ceremony to enter a monastery.
  - The novice must be free from debt and know the passages to recite at the ceremony.
  - Before the ceremony he will visit the wat, make offerings and ring the gong.
  - The day before the ceremony he walks in a procession wearing white, with his head shaved – symbols of purity.
  - On his initiation day he circles the wat four times wearing rich clothing and carrying incense, a candle and a lotus.
  - He removes the rich clothing and throws coins on floor as symbols of leaving the worldly life behind like Siddhartha Gautama (the Buddha).
  - He enters the ordination hall and asks to be admitted.
  - The abbot asks him questions and he must answer in Pali.
  - Finally he puts on yellow robes and begins life as monk.

Christianity

- The confirmation ceremony at around twelve years of age confirms the promises made for the young person at Baptism:
  - The young person attends preparation classes.
  - The service is conducted by a bishop, who asks candidates the three questions asked at birth, to which they respond yes.
  - He lays hands on their forehead and confirms their commitment to the Church.
  - Holy Communion is then celebrated, and confirmation candidates take first communion.
- The Baptist Church has a Believer's Baptism:
  - Candidates make confession of sins and confirm acceptance of Christ as saviour.
  - The minister leads them into the baptistry, they are fully immersed under the water, which symbolises dying to sin and rising to life again in Christ.

Hinduism

- Hindus celebrate the Sacred Thread Ceremony for boys at around twelve years, which symbolises full entry into their caste.
  - It takes place in a garden around a sacred fire.
  - Puja (worship) is conducted by the boy's teacher who presents him with a sacred thread, which is placed over his left shoulder across the body to the right hip.
  - The boy is now allowed to conduct religious ceremonies, recite scripture and marry.

Islam

- There is no initiation ceremony as the child is a Muslim from birth.
- At the age of four children take part in a Bismillah Ceremony:
  - It remembers the Prophet Muhammad (pbuh) receiving the revelations from angel Jibrail.
  - The child learns the Bismillah passage from the Qur'an, which is recited at the ceremony to family and friends.
  - Gifts are received and celebrations follow – marks beginning of religious education.

Judaism

- The Bar Mitzvah ceremony for boys is at the age of thirteen; the Bat Mitzvah ceremony for girls is at age twelve. Each ceremony symbolises the move from childhood to adulthood.
  - The title means 'Son of the Commandments' ('Daughter' for girls).
  - A period of training and preparation with the Rabbi takes place before the ceremony.
  - The ceremony takes place in synagogue on the Sabbath nearest to the thirteenth birthday.
  - Torah scrolls are prepared at the Bimah by the Rabbi, and the boy is invited to come and read passages in Hebrew.
  - Sermon is then given by the Rabbi and the boy is blessed – he is now obligated to keep all of the commandments.
  - Celebrations follow.

Sikhism

- Initiation into the Khalsa can be made at any age, usually from around twelve onwards.
- The Amrit Ceremony initiates Sikhs into full membership of the Sikh Khalsa.
  - The ceremony is conducted in front of the Guru Granth Sahib with five Khalsa Sikhs dressed to represent the Panj Pyare.
  - Amrit is stirred with a khanda – a double-edged sword.
  - The granthi recites passages from the Guru Granth Sahib and one of the Khalsa members recites the vows the initiates must promise to keep.
  - Initiates kneel on one knee showing readiness to defend faith.
  - Amrit is sprinkled on their hair and eyes, and all drink from same bowl showing equality.
  - Prayers and hymns follow, then the ceremony ends with sharing of Karah Parshad.
  - Men take the name Singh (meaning lion), women Kaur (meaning princess).

Exam tip

Learn the order of the ceremony and the important words, actions and objects that are used in the ceremony. Use these to write detailed accounts of what happens in a ceremony. You only need to know one birth ceremony and one commitment ceremony; you will never be asked to write about more than this.

Key term

Ceremonies of commitment – religious rituals performed to celebrate a child's move to adulthood within a faith; these can also be initiation ceremonies in some faiths

Why are ceremonies of commitment important?

Revised

When children are growing up their **parents take responsibility** for their religious instruction. In the home they **learn the important beliefs and duties** of following the religious faith. There comes a time when children need to **decide for themselves** that they wish to follow the lifestyle expected of a believer in the faith. These ceremonies **mark the transition from being a child to being a full adult member** of the religion. In preparing for the ceremony they will have **undergone instruction** and teaching about their religion. They will have **thought deeply** about what it is they believe and value. The ceremony gives them the **opportunity to announce to all** that they want to live according to the rules of their faith.

Exam tip

The words and phrases in bold are to aid your revision.

Common mistakes

Some candidates confuse ceremonies of commitment with birth ceremonies. You need to make sure you are clear about the difference between them.

Revised

Topic basics 3: Young people and religion

How do young people make moral choices? ──────── Revised ☐

Influences on young people

- Upbringing – including parents, other family, environment.
- **Spirituality** – inner personal conscience and awareness.
- **Moral codes** – the law, family values, religious teachings, personal values.
- Religious beliefs – influence on development, choice to maintain faith.
- **Peer pressure** – need to fit in with group, conform to accepted norms of group.
- Other influences – education, the law, culture, media, **secular society**.

> **Key terms**
>
> **Spirituality** – a sense of awe and wonder, something outside of everyday human experience
>
> **Moral codes** – rules about morality which influence the way people live their lives
>
> **Peer pressure** – the influence of friends on each other
>
> **Secular society** – all aspects of society that are not connected with or influenced by religion

> **Exam tip**
>
> Make sure that you are clear on which influences are religious and which are secular.

Rights and responsibilities ──────── Revised ☐

Everyone in society is entitled to **rights**. Young people have a right to things like an education, fair treatment, protection of the law and so on. But all people have **responsibilities**, duties that they should fulfil. When people do not live up to their responsibilities they may find that their rights and freedoms are taken away. So we uphold the law and obey it in order to be protected by it. Young people's rights are enshrined in the law and in the Declaration of the Rights of the Child.

> **Key terms**
>
> **Rights** – entitlements that all people should have
>
> **Responsibilities** – duties that a person has to others, their faith, etc.
>
> **Generation gap** – a difference between the views of young people and their elders

Freedom of choice

This is the idea that we have freedom of choice in our decisions and actions. However:

- there are always limitations to free choice, e.g. the law, age, parental restrictions, religious obligations, restrictions on work
- the **generation gap** can lead to conflict between young people and older members of society
- religions impose rules on people with the need to obey to save their own soul, even though they all say we have free will
- peer groups impose rules by expecting us to behave in certain ways.

Being religious

Faith groups – activities for young people

- Worship – youth services, ceremonies for birth and commitment, religious instruction.
- Festivals – fun for children, stories, celebrations, gifts.
- Youth organisations – Scout and Guide Movement, Boys/Girls Brigade.
- Religious holidays – Taizé, retreats, community sponsored breaks.
- Social activities – youth clubs, sport and recreation, prayer groups.
- Voluntary work – gap year activities, sponsored events, participation in community.

Benefits for young believers

- Range of activities.
- Membership and belonging.
- Sense of meaning and purpose.
- **Empowerment** – having certainty in beliefs and lifestyle can instil confidence.
- Support of **brotherhood** and sisterhood.

Problems for young believers

Young people can find that their religious beliefs make it difficult to always 'fit in'.

- Secular society conflicts such as dress and popular culture.
- **Marginalisation** – social process of exclusion and being left out.
- Peer pressure – lack of acceptance of faith and misunderstanding.
- Discrimination – religious prejudice leading to discrimination.
- Generation gap – conflict between young people and their elders due to misunderstanding, contrasting values, etc.

> **Common mistakes**
>
> Many candidates assume that following a religion is forced on young people and that it limits their freedom. You need to be objective. There are many young people who choose to follow a religious faith because it benefits them socially, emotionally and spiritually.
>

> **Key terms**
>
> **Empowerment** – developing confidence in individuals or groups
>
> **Brotherhood** – support derived by being part of a community with shared values, aspirations, etc. (sisterhood is the female form of this)
>
> **Marginalisation** – the social process of becoming isolated and left out; it can affect individuals and groups

Role of schools

State schools

- Religious Studies (all schools must teach this).
- **Assemblies** (collective worship).

Faith schools

- Differences to state schools, e.g. admissions, rules based on the faith principles of the students' families.
- Reasons for **faith schools**, e.g. to educate within the context of the faith, maintain the faith through observation of traditions, dress codes and religious teachings.
- Reasons against faith schools, e.g. they can be thought to promote segregation, prejudice and deny full education of other faiths.

> **Key terms**
>
> **Assemblies** – occasions where students are brought together in schools for collective worship
>
> **Faith schools** – schools that are supported by a specific faith group; the school ethos and curriculum reflects the beliefs of that faith

Religious teachings on religion and young people: good teachings to learn

Revised

Buddhism

- In the Rahula Sutta the Buddha instructs his son of the importance of learning from his mistakes.
- 'Neither fire nor wind, birth nor death can erase our good deeds' (Buddha).
- 'We are what we think. All that we are arises with our thoughts. With our thoughts, we make our world' (Buddha).
- 'Morality, compassion, decency, wisdom, these qualities must be taught through moral education in a social environment, so that a more humane world may emerge' (Dalai Lama).
- 'Teaching our children the dharma is the best way to safeguard their minds and hearts from the many unwholesome and negative influences of our modern society' (Buddhist Faith Fellowship).

Christianity

- Spare the rod, spoil the child (Proverbs 13:24).
- Suffer the little children to come unto me, and forbid them not: for of such is the kingdom of God (Mark).
- Run from anything that gives you the evil thoughts that young men often have, but stay close to anything that makes you want to do right (II Timothy 2:22).
- Don't let anyone look down on you because you are young, but set an example for the believers in speech, in life, in love, in faith and in purity (I Timothy 4:12).
- Children, obey your parents in everything, for this pleases the Lord (Colossians 3:20).

Sikhism

- In this world of her parents' home, she may come to know the Giver of peace (Guru Granth Sahib).
- Gazing upon the tiny bodies of your children, love has welled up within your heart; you are proud of them (Guru Granth Sahib).
- The faithful uplift and redeem their family and relations (Guru Granth Sahib).
- Duty to the One Lord is upon the heads of all (Guru Granth Sahib).
- You are born and you come out, and your mother and father are delighted to see your face (Guru Granth Sahib).

All religions teach:
- religious duty
- continue the faith
- rites of passage

Hinduism

- 'I have seen children successfully overcoming the effects of an evil inheritance due to purity being an inherent attribute of the soul' (Mohandas Gandhi).
- 'A man in this world without learning, is as a beast of the field' (Hindu proverb).
- 'Action is greater than inaction. Perform your task in life' (Bhagavad Gita).
- The evil deeds of those who destroy the family tradition and give rise to unwanted children, destroy community projects and family welfare' (Bhagavad Gita).
- Ganesha is particularly important for young people as he is the God of intelligence.

Judaism

- Honour your father and mother (Exodus 20:12).
- Don't let the excitement of being young cause you to forget about your Creator: Honour Him in your youth (Ecclesiastes 12:1).
- Do not withhold correction from a child, beat him with a rod and deliver his soul from hell (Proverbs).
- Listen, my son, to your father's instruction and do not forsake your mother's teaching (Proverbs 1:8).
- When my father and my mother forsake me, then the LORD will take me up (Psalm 27:10).

Islam

- 'Be good to your parents' (Qur'an 6:151).
- The Prophet Muhammad (pbuh) said that paradise lies at the feet of your mother (Hadith).
- Those who show the most perfect faith are kindest to their families (Hadith).
- When asked which acts were most good, the Prophet replied first prayer and second duty to parents (Hadith).
- The Prophet warned that those who did not care for their parents would not enter paradise (Hadith).

What questions on this topic look like:
Religion and young people

Check back to pages 11–12 to see the grids examiners use to mark questions worth three or more marks.

This page contains a range of examples of questions that could be on an exam paper for this topic. Practise them all to strengthen your knowledge and technique while revising. Check the website for answers to some of these, with tips.

1   Give **one** advantage of schools having an assembly.   [1]
2   What is a moral code?   [1]
3   Give **two** different influences on young people as they grow up.   [2]
4   Explain what is meant by the generation gap.   [2]
5   Give **two** faith activities for young religious believers.   [2]
6   Describe an initiation ceremony in one religion you have studied.   [3]
7   Explain why a young person may be a member of a faith group.   [3]
8   'Faith schools are the best choice for children from religious families.' What do you think? Explain your opinion.   [3]
9   Explain the rights and responsibilities of young people in a faith group.   [4]
10 Describe some of the ways that faith groups can encourage young people to join.   [4]
11 Explain **two** reasons why some parents choose to send their children to a faith school.   [4]
12 Explain the birth ceremonies in **one** religion you have studied.   [5]
13 Explain how the influences on young people can affect their life choices.   [5]
14 Explain the advantages and disadvantages for young people who have religious faith.   [5]
15 'There is no point to ceremonies of commitment.' Do you agree? Give reasons for your answer, showing that you have thought about more than one point of view. Refer to religious arguments in your answer.   [6]
16 'Parents should not make their children follow a specific religion.' Do you agree? Give reasons for your answer, showing that you have thought about more than one point of view. Refer to religious arguments in your answer.   [6]
17 'Religion is too old fashioned for young people today.' Do you agree? Give reasons for your answer, showing that you have thought about more than one point of view. Refer to religious arguments in your answer.   [6]

Online

Exam tip

It is often difficult to use teachings directly for this topic, so get used to using the general concepts, e.g. a question about how religious believers should bring up their children can be answered by saying they have a duty to teach them the faith, etc.

Exam tip

Did you know an F-grade candidate will rarely write in a way that makes clear what they mean? Their answers may be brief and often not actually answering the question that they have been asked. Learning information will help this.

Did you know that a C-grade candidate often knows and understands a lot of their course material. However, they do not use this well in their answers, often repeating points or not focusing on the specifics of the question asked. Their answers can be overlong and they sometimes run out of time and do not complete all the questions. Practice is crucial.

Did you know that an A-grade candidate writes clear and precise answers to the questions asked. They structure their responses clearly and avoid repetition of points. They will time their answers to allow them to read through and check before the end of the exam.

So, which one are you?

Religion and Morality (AQA B Unit 3 40553)

Topic 1 Religious attitudes to medical ethics

Key knowledge

- Know why people choose to have or not to have children.
- Know different types of fertility treatment.
- Understand why people seek fertility treatment.
- Religious attitudes to:
  - life
  - fertility treatments (IVF, AID, AIH, surrogacy)
  - medical research (cloning, genetic engineering, stem cell therapies, experimentation)
  - medical support to improve life (transplants, transfusions).

Topic basics 1: Life

When does life begin?
Revised

Some believe life begins at **conception** – when the egg and sperm (and soul) meet. For others, it is when the **child is born**. Between those two, people say it is when the **primitive streak** appears (at fifteen days), or when the foetus would be **able to survive if born** (around 24 weeks). For Muslims, it is at ensoulment (when the soul enters the foetus) which is around 120 days.

> **Exam tip**
>
> The words and phrases in bold are key ideas for you to learn. They will make your answers stronger in the exam if you learn them and practise using them.

Sanctity of life
Revised

All religions, and people generally, think life is special or sacred; they believe in the **sanctity of life**. Maybe because **God made** it as the **most important part of creation**, or because it carries a **soul or anatta** which moves through incarnations, or it carries the **highest value in law**.

> **Key term**
>
> **Sanctity of life** – the belief that life is special or sacred, because God made it, or because of the soul or anatta

Creating life – whose right?

Revised

 Christianity, Judaism, and Islam teach that …

God **plans** a life for each of us, and **blesses** couples with children. It is up to God that someone should be born.

 Buddhism, Hinduism, and Sikhism teach that …

Children are a **blessing** for a couple. Each **new life is a new chance** for a soul or anatta to pay off bad and accumulate good karma in its journey to Nirvana or enlightenment.

Non-religious people might say it is entirely up to the individuals concerned, with input from their families and doctors.

> **Exam tip**
>
> It is important to remember these different ideas, because it affects attitudes to whether we can help with fertility and what we can do to an embryo and a foetus.

Maintaining life/medical science

Revised

 Christianity, Judaism, and Islam teach that …

God gave man stewardship and dominion over the creation which means we have to look after others. The Sirach (Apocrypha, a part of the Bible) says God gives man medical knowledge.

 Buddhism, Hinduism, and Sikhism teach that …

By helping others, we acquire good karma which helps in future lifetimes.

Doctors take the Hippocratic Oath to preserve life. So we have a duty to use medicine to look after others. The issue is how far we can go with this duty. We can see that cloning an organ like a liver is helpful, but how helpful is cloning a human, for example?

> **Exam tip**
>
> These provide reasons for supporting medical science – remember 'intention to help'.

Topic basics 2: Fertility treatment

Fertility treatments are medical interventions to aid pregnancy. They give childless couples a chance to have children, and so fulfil any duty to reproduce. Many treatments allow couples to have children of their own blood. However, all enable non-traditional families to have children as well (single people, same-sex couples), which is a controversial issue for some people.

> **Key term**
>
> **Fertility treatment** – medical treatment to help a woman become pregnant, for example IVF, AIH, AID

In-vitro fertilisation (IVF)

Revised

During **IVF** treatment eggs and sperm from the couple are mixed in a petri dish, which enables many of the eggs to become fertilised. After several days a viable embryo is selected and implanted into the woman's womb. This type of treatment is used when there are no problems with the eggs and sperm but they are unable to become fertilised naturally.

The treatment can also be performed using donor eggs and/or sperm for couples having further difficulties conceiving.

Children born using this treatment can be referred to as 'test tube babies' due to the way the eggs are fertilised.

> **Key term**
>
> **IVF** – in-vitro fertilisation – the practice of fertilising an egg in a petri dish, which is then implanted into the womb; it is a non-sexual process for pregnancy

Pros and cons

+ Basically it is just a process to assist couples to become pregnant.

− It is an expensive process, unavailable to many.

− There is a low success rate (around 25 per cent).

− Using donor materials may be seen as adultery.

− A high number of embryos are destroyed.

AIH and AID

Revised

AIH and AID mean artificial insemination by the husband (H) or donor (D) respectively. Sperm is collected (via masturbation) and artificially placed high into the woman's womb to increase the chances of egg and sperm meeting and fertilising.

Pros and cons

+ The process can allow childless couples to have *their own* children.

+ If the man is infertile or carrying a genetic illness, it still allows the couple to have a child by donor.

− There is a low success rate (around 20 per cent).

− Using donor materials may be seen as adultery.

− There are potential problems over knowing the 'real' father when the child is older.

> **Key term**
>
> **AIH or AID** – artificial insemination by husband or donor

> **Common mistakes**
>
> Some candidates confuse AID (fertility treatment) with AIDS (illness). Obviously any answer about AIDS would be completely wrong – it isn't even a subject on this exam (which is how you could remember not to write about it!).
>
> Revised

Surrogacy

Revised

Sometimes a woman is unable to carry a pregnancy to full term. It may be she repeatedly miscarries, or has had her womb removed, for example. **Surrogacy** is when a couple ask another woman to become pregnant (with their own or a donor egg and/or sperm) usually through artificial means. She then takes the pregnancy to full term and hands the baby over for them to bring up as their own.

Pros and cons

+ The process can allow childless couples to have *their own* children.

+ Where a woman cannot become or stay pregnant, this still allows the couple to have a child.

− It is illegal to be a paid surrogate in the UK.

− Using donor material (even a donor womb) could be seen as adultery.

− There are potential social issues of who the real mother is, and how the child will respond when it knows its own origins.

> **Key term**
>
> **Surrogacy** – where a couple are helped to have a child by another woman; the second woman (the surrogate) is made pregnant (usually by artificial means), takes the pregnancy to full term, and then returns the baby to the couple

> **Exam tip**
>
> When writing about attitudes to these treatments, try to contrast the intention (to help, to use medical knowledge from God kindly) with the procedures (no sexual intercourse, use of donor materials, destruction of embryos). Apply teachings to these.

Topic basics 3: Helping medicine

The term 'helping medicine' generally refers to **blood transfusions** and **organ transplants**. Few, if any, people – religious believers or not – disagree with these procedures, because they save life, and are now a universal form of medical treatment in every hospital in the world. In fact, they are a significant part of hospital work. Religious believers all believe we should help each other, and that we have a duty to look after the sick. Both transfusions and transplants are genuine acts of compassion and kindness as the person donating has no idea who they will be helping.

> **Key terms**
>
> **Blood transfusion** – the giving/receiving of matched blood for medical purposes, e.g. receiving blood as part of an operation
>
> **Organ transplant** – operation to replace a faulty organ, e.g. kidney transplant

> **Exam tip**
>
> Think about whether religious believers should both accept *and* donate blood and organs, given they are supposed to help others. Know the teachings that support helping, and those that work against it.

Blood transfusion

Revised

There are many medical reasons for receiving a blood transfusion, for example, to replace lost blood, during surgery, to treat certain inherited blood disorders. Each person has to be given blood that matches their own, i.e. it is the same blood group. The National Blood Donor Service is always asking for people to donate blood, as supplies are always too low. Few people would reject a blood transfusion, although Jehovah's Witnesses do because in Genesis (Bible) it says that 'the life is in the blood' and this prohibits them from taking in any blood, including by transfusion.

Common mistakes

Some candidates write about Jehovah's Witnesses saying the *soul* is in the blood and that by transfusing blood a soul is being transfused. This is wrong – and will receive no marks.

Revised

Organ transplantation

Revised

Our organs can get damaged and their function become impaired or lost for many reasons. Where this is irreparable, our **quality of life** is affected, and we could die. It is possible to have an organ transplant in this case, if a suitable organ is available which is also a tissue match. There are waiting lists for most organs, as they are usually only available when someone dies, if they have agreed to donate organs, if the organs are still viable, and if they are a match. Once transplanted, the recipient faces a lifetime of medication to make sure their body doesn't reject the organ.

Xenotransplantation

Xenotransplantation is the use of organs from animals in place of human organs. A common example is the use of a heart valve from a pig. Since 1995, doctors have been using genetically modified animals. This has increased the number of organs available, though they do not last as long as human organs so are often used as a stop-gap until a human organ is available.

Key terms

Quality of life – how good someone's life is based on their physical or mental health

Xenotransplantation – transplants using animal parts, e.g. the valve from the heart of a pig in heart surgery

Medical research – medical studies to generate new medicines and procedures to support life, and to further understanding of how the body works

Topic basics 4: Frankenstein sciences

Exam tip

Think about it – why are people so nervous about these medical advances? This type of question is common as an evaluative question.

Medical research has moved on from treating illness to trying to prevent it in the first place. In the last twenty years, laws have had to be passed to regulate research so that it is not unethical. It includes genetic modification, stem cell therapies and cloning – so far. Many people are very nervous about these medical advances, wondering whether they are a step too far.

The Human Embryo and Fertilisation Act (1990)

Revised

This Act covers three areas:

- It regulates any fertility treatment using donated eggs and/or sperm, and embryos created through IVF.
- It makes rules about storage of eggs, sperm and embryos.
- It gives guidelines for **experiments involving humans**.

In 2000 and 2001, the Act was amended to allow the use of a dead man's sperm, stored before death, and to allow doctors to create embryos for therapeutic cloning. This was about improving medicine for the future, and better understanding of disease.

Key term

Experiments on humans – medical experiments using human subjects in order to test medicines, for example

Embryology

Revised

Embryology is **research of and into embryos**. It involves the **creation of embryos artificially** (often the remnants from fertility treatment are used) and **dissecting, observing and testing** on them. It is done to **better understand very early life**, in order to support it, and to **better understand pregnancy**, in order to make it safer. All embryos not destroyed in the process of research have to be **destroyed before fourteen days** (day fifteen is the primitive streak and the next stage of development). Each of those embryos was a **potential life**, which is the biggest problem for most people against this type of work.

Pros and cons

+ The research is giving important information to better understand very early pregnancy.

+ It is helping to better understand very early foetal development.

+ It makes good use of embryos that would otherwise have been destroyed.

– Ultimately it destroys every embryo created.

> ### Key term
>
> **Embryology** – research using embryos (up to fourteen days old) in order to improve knowledge about pregnancy and the beginnings of life

> ### Exam tip
>
> The words and phrases in bold are key ideas for you to learn. They will make your answers stronger in the exam if you learn them and practise using them.

Genetic engineering on humans

Revised

Genetic engineering is the removal, swapping or altering of genetic structures within an embryo, before it is implanted for pregnancy. It is aimed at fighting genetic illnesses, which can strike from birth or later in life. There are now more than 250 gene protocols coming from this work to alleviate suffering. This work is very tightly monitored and regulated because of concerns about misuse of the knowledge.

Pros and cons

+ It is fighting some illnesses before they even get started.

+ It is improving the chances and quality of life for some people.

+ It may eradicate some serious genetic illnesses.

– Destruction of embryos is part of the process.

– Huge costs are involved.

– Some people believe this is 'playing God'.

– Researchers are not yet sure about possible long-term consequences of this work.

> ### Key term
>
> **Genetic engineering** – the removal or swapping of genetic material within embryos to try to remove the likelihood for a disease or illness

> ### Exam tip
>
> If you don't know the terms, you can't answer the questions – so learn them. You don't need to know much scientific detail, because it is an RS exam.

Stem cell research

Revised

Stem cells are found in embryos and in every human. They are easiest to harvest from embryos and the umbilical cord. They are cells that have the ability to transform into any type of cell, and are how an embryo develops into a full human being with all its different aspects and organs. In **stem cell research** they are being used to 'grow' organs such as kidneys (which could be used in transplant surgery), and to help repair parts of the body (e.g. areas of the brain in people with Parkinson's Disease).

> ### Key term
>
> **Stem cell research** – research using stem cells, usually from embryos and umbilical cords; stem cells have the ability to become any type of cells; used in treatment of illness

Pros and cons

+ This process could provide an alternative to harvesting organs from dead people.

+ It is improving the chances and quality of life for some people.

− Destruction of embryos is part of the process.

− Huge costs are involved.

− Some people believe this is 'playing God'.

Human cloning

Revised

Human cloning is creating an exact DNA copy of a person. An embryo is created then its DNA is removed to be replaced with DNA from the person to be cloned. Having applied an electrical charge, the embryo begins to develop normally. Animals have been cloned; however, it is illegal across the whole world to clone humans.

> **Key term**
>
> **Human cloning** – the creation of an exact DNA replica of a person

Therapeutic cloning

This is the cloning of tissues or organs to replace failing ones in a person. Its aim is to provide an organ that the body will not reject, so reducing the need for medication for life.

Pros and cons

+ Therapeutic cloning would massively improve the success rate of organ transplantation.

+ It should improve the chances and quality of life for some people.

− Destruction of embryos is part of the process.

− Huge costs are involved.

− Some people believe this is 'playing God'.

− There seems to be no point in making an exact DNA copy of a whole person.

− The clone's cellular age is the same as that of the donor, and so early onset illnesses linked to ageing are normal (e.g. arthritis, diabetes, etc.). So, for example, Dolly the sheep had a cellular age of a much older animal.

Experimentation on humans

Revised

This is done in behavioural studies, but more controversially for medicine testing. All those involved are volunteers and paid well for their time. It is necessary to finally test new drugs on humans before releasing them for use, because no animal test results will be the same as on humans. You tend to know about these only when they go wrong – then they hit the headlines! Many people still recall news of experimentation done by the Nazis in the Second World War, and so feel concern about this. However, there is heavy regulation to prevent abuse by doctors in experiments.

> **Exam tip**
>
> For each, you need to know a simple description of what they are, how they can help humans, and why some people have concerns. This knowledge allows you to answer any question, and by adding some religious teachings like 'Love your neighbour', you justify the use of something to help others, or by using one like 'God has a plan for each of us', you justify disagreeing with something.

Pros and cons

+ People are involved by choice; they are not forced.

+ It gives us reliable results and indicators for medicines which can then be used to help people.

− There is a fear regarding abuse of the system by doctors.

Religious teachings on religious attitudes to medical ethics: good teachings to learn

Revised

Buddhism

- Life exists from conception, when egg, sperm and anatta combine.
- First Precept – Help, not harm, others.
- Metta and compassion for all sentient beings.
- The Bodhisattva Vow – help other beings.
- 'Cherish in your hearts boundless goodwill to all beings' (Buddha).

Sikhism

- May you have seven sons – a traditional wedding blessing.
- Life begins at conception, and is given by God as an expression of his will.
- Any third person within a marriage is seen as adultery, so is wrong.
- Through selfless service, eternal peace is obtained (Guru Granth Sahib).
- The true servants of God are those who serve Him through helping others (Guru Granth Sahib).

Christianity

- Go forth and multiply (Genesis).
- God knows each of us intimately, and has set a plan for our life (Psalms).
- Following Natural Law means to accept the will of God re fertility (Roman Catholic teaching).
- God has given doctors their wisdom (Apocrypha).
- Jesus' example of helping others should be followed.

All religions teach:
- sanctity of life
- miracle of life
- quality of life
- fidelity
- forgiveness

Judaism

- Go forth and multiply (Genesis).
- The Tenakh has several stories of women being helped to conceive (e.g. 2 Kings 4:14–16).
- God gave doctors their medical knowledge (Sirach/Apocrypha).
- If one is in the position to be able to donate an organ to save another's life, it is obligatory to do so (Rabbi Moses Tendler).
- It is forbidden to mutilate a body, and the whole body must be buried.

Islam

- Allah gives life to who he chooses (Qur'an).
- Do not come near adultery or fornication for it is shameful (Qur'an).
- Having children is seen as a duty for Muslims.
- Whoever saves a life, it would be as if he had saved the life of all people (Qur'an).
- Shari'ah Law prohibits the mutilation of a body.

Hinduism

- The householder (grihastha) stage of life should lead to children in a family.
- Life begins at conception when egg, sperm and soul combine.
- All men come into this world burdened by ancestor debt. This is repaid by fathering a son (Pitri-rin).
- Fertility treatments that use material from a third person in karma are similar to adultery so are wrong.
- Daya (compassion) and dana (charity) must be practised by all Hindus.

Common mistakes

Many candidates just list teachings and/or beliefs, and let the examiner make sense of them for the question – it means they get lower marks. For example, if you say 'Sikhs believe in sewa (service)', you need to say why that is relevant to the question.

Revised

Exam tip

Candidates who use specific teachings make their answers clearer, and get better marks.

What questions on this topic look like:
Religious attitudes to matters of life (medical ethics)

Check back to pages 11–12 to see the grids examiners use to mark questions worth three or more marks.

This page contains a range of examples of questions that could be on an exam paper for this topic. Practise them all to strengthen your knowledge and technique while revising. Check the website for answers to some of these, with tips.

1 What is IVF? [1]

2 What is meant by surrogacy? [1]

3 What is meant by blood transfusion? [1]

4 Give **two** reasons why some religious believers agree with AIH. [2]

5 Explain what is meant by *transplant surgery*. [2]

6 Give **two** types of fertility treatment. [2]

7 Explain briefly why religious believers think life is sacred. [3]

8 Explain religious attitudes to genetic engineering on humans. [3]

9 'All religious believers should donate organs for transplants.' What do you think? Explain your opinion. [3]

10 Explain religious attitudes to fertility treatment. You may refer to beliefs and teachings in your answer. [4]

11 Explain why some religious believers disagree with stem cell research. [4]

12 Explain why some religious believers agree with experiments on humans. [4]

13 Explain how belief in the sanctity of life affects attitudes to embryology. [5]

14 Using religious beliefs and teachings, explain religious attitudes to cloning. [5]

15 Explain why some religious believers agree with surrogacy. [5]

16 'Fertility treatment is an expensive waste of money.' Do you agree? Give reasons for your answer, showing you have thought about more than one point of view. Refer to religious arguments in your answer. [6]

17 'People who cannot have children should just accept it.' Do you agree? Give reasons for your answer, showing you have thought about more than one point of view. Refer to religious arguments in your answer. [6]

18 'Genetic engineering is playing God.' Do you agree? Give reasons for your answer, showing you have thought about more than one point of view. Refer to religious arguments in your answer. [6]

Online

Exam tip

If you look at exam papers or the practice exam questions for this book on the website, you'll see that each set of questions starts with a 'picture stimulus'.

Did you know that F-grade candidates don't try to see any answers in the picture stimulus? The picture stimulus should give you some answers or ideas for at least the first part of the question. A lot of the weakest candidates seem to think they are there for decoration or for colouring in!

Did you know that C-grade candidates do make some use of the stimulus – if it is really obvious. The answer might refer to the stimulus or the subject of the stimulus, and this helps them to get a better understanding of the topic.

Did you know that A-grade candidates routinely use stimulus and refer to them in their answers. They use them as an example to write about, or to help understand the question when they feel a bit stuck. The examiner puts the stimulus in precisely to help the candidate – take the time to take a look.

So, which one are you?

Topic 2 Religious attitudes to the elderly and death

- What religions believe about life after death.
- What euthanasia is.
- Reasons to agree or disagree with euthanasia.
- Religious attitudes to:
  - euthanasia
  - life support
  - hospices
  - caring for the dying.
- The right to decide on euthanasia.
- The argument for hospices.
- How the elderly can be supported.

Topic basics 1: The elderly

Age for **retirement** in the UK is generally 65, but this will be higher in the future. This is the age by which people can currently claim a state pension, which should mean they do not have to work. More and more people are choosing to continue to work because they need more money than their pension gives them, and because they still want and feel able to work. 'The **elderly**' is a term we can use for those who have retired; however, many people of that age in developed countries do not see themselves as elderly, as it makes them sound in need of support in some way (and many aren't until much older).

Key terms

Retirement – the point at which a person stops working for their living

Elderly – people over a certain age, perhaps 65–70 and older

Problems faced by the elderly

Revised

- **Ageism** – people discriminating against them because of their age, for example, taking advantage, bullying, assuming they can't do something, forcing retirement.
- Health issues – as we age, our body and brain become less efficient. Many elderly people have more problems with ill-health, and many illnesses are age-related, e.g. diabetes, arthritis. Worsening mobility is often an issue.
- Financial problems – the state pension is not huge, and many elderly people struggle to live comfortably on just that.
- **Death** – the loss of friends and family as others age with them, but also concerns about their own death which is closer as they get older – what will happen to their body, to them, to their family.
- Loneliness – their partner may have died, they may live away from their family or have no family and few or no friends left.
- Mental health issues – dementia and Alzheimer's are age-related.

Key terms

Ageism – prejudice against people because of their age

Death – the end of life, usually confirmed by the brain stem no longer functioning

Caring for the elderly

Many elderly people **do not need any support**; they can look after themselves well, have enough money, have friends and family, and live very fulfilled lives. Some will do voluntary work in their community and abroad.

Some elderly people need help from their families – perhaps taking them shopping, etc. However, they are **self-reliant** in almost every way.

Some elderly people need to **access support services** from local government, e.g. Meals on Wheels, community centre afternoons. They can still live in their own homes. Some of these people need home help, which means someone is paid to go and check on them and do small jobs for them several times a week.

Some live in **sheltered accommodation**, which means they are close to support through a warden system. They may access other government support as part of this.

Some live in **care homes for the elderly**. They are often unable to look after themselves fully, and so need this 24/7 support.

Common mistakes

Candidates often write about the elderly as if they are helpless (and useless!). However, many are doing as much as they did before retirement, it is just that they aren't getting paid. Their **quality of life** hasn't changed at all (if anything it is often better!). Your examiner might be 'elderly', so mind what you say!

Exam tip

The words and phrases in bold are key ideas for you to learn. They will make your answers stronger in the exam if you learn them and practise using them.

Exam tip

Why should religious believers look after the elderly? The same reasons anyone else would, for a start – they are family, they looked after us, etc. You can use secular answers, but need to know some religious ones as well.

Key terms

Care home – home for the elderly where their needs are catered for day and night

Quality of life – how good someone's life is based on their physical or mental health

Topic basics 2: Life after death

Life after death

Buddhism

Buddhists believe in **rebirth**. There is **no permanent soul**, rather a mix of ever-changing skandhas – emotions, feelings, intelligence and so on. After the death of the body, this mix fuses with an egg and sperm at conception. The **thoughts, actions and intentions** of each life shape the quality of the next. The goal is to **achieve enlightenment**, and stop being reborn.

Christianity

Christians believe in the **physical resurrection** of the body. At death, the body waits until **Judgement Day**. Catholics call this Purgatory. At judgement, a person faces God and Jesus to evaluate their deeds. If they were **good** in life, they go to **heaven**, which is paradise and wonderful forever. If they were **bad**, they go to **hell** for eternal punishment.

Islam

Muslims believe in **resurrection**. At death, the body waits in the grave (**barzakh**) and sees the events of its life. This can be quick or very slow and painful. On **Judgement Day**, people are sorted according to their beliefs and actions. The **wicked** are cast into **hell**; the **truly good** go **straight to Paradise**. All others cross **As-Sirat bridge**, carrying the book of their deeds (sins make it heavier). The bridge is sharp, and so they are **purified** from sin before going to Paradise.

Sikhism

Sikhs believe in **reincarnation**. The soul is born into **many lifetimes**, whose quality is decided by the **words, thoughts and deeds** of the previous lifetime(s). The point of each life is to **serve and worship God**, so that eventually the soul can be **reunited with God** (waheguru) and stop being reincarnated.

Judaism

Judaism **focuses on this life**, rather than the next. **Some teachings mention a heavenly place**. Jews talk of the 'world to come', which is when the **Messiah will come to rule the earth in peace**. That is **life after death** because the **dead will be woken to live through that time**.

Hinduism

Hindus believe in **reincarnation**. Their **atman** (soul) lives through many lifetimes, each one shaped by the **thoughts, words and actions** of their past lifetime(s). Its goal is to **achieve enlightenment** and become one with the Ultimate Reality, so stopping being reincarnated.

> **Key term**
>
> **Life after death** – belief that after death, we will have life again, either through resurrection, rebirth or reincarnation

> **Exam tips**
>
> - Learn the key points for each of two religions. When asking for beliefs about life after death, there are three or four marks. Two quick lists of key points will get you full marks every time.
> - This topic can come up as an evaluative question – is there really such a thing as life after death? Think about arguments for and against – these teachings are one argument for.
> - How might believing in life after death affect the way you live life now? You need to think about that.

Topic basics 3: Caring for the dying

> **Exam tip**
>
> Should we have the right to die? How should the dying be cared for? For the exam you need to be able to answer both.

Everyone dies – we all know that. For some, that death is sudden, or swift. For others, it comes at the end of a long and/or painful time.

Some people die at home with family, having been looked after by family. If they have a **terminal illness**, they are likely to be supported by organisations such as Macmillan Nurses (cancer) as well as the NHS.

> **Key term**
>
> **Terminal illness** – illness that will lead to death, and that cannot be cured

The hospice movement   Revised ☐

Hospices are homes for the dying. Christians set up the first hospices in the Middle Ages; Sikh gurus set up hospices – religions clearly feel a need to help the dying (who often have no one else to help them). Hospices provide specialist care. They differ from hospitals because:

> **Key term**
>
> **Hospice** – a place where the terminally ill can be cared for in their last days

- patients don't recover – they are terminally ill and on average stay only two weeks in a hospice before they die
- the money to run hospices comes from charity
- there are many more professionals for the number of patients than in hospitals
- hospices try to care for all of a person's needs – not just to relieve physical symptoms of an illness.

How hospices help their patients

> **Common mistakes**
>
> When asked what a hospice is, many candidates answer that it is a care home for the elderly or a hospital. Neither answer is correct. Hospices care for the dying – learn it.
>
> Revised ☐

- Nurses use any means to get rid of pain, including massage and therapies.
- They care for the emotional and spiritual well-being of the patient – many are confused and angry as to why this is happening to them; they also worry about their family, and the items they leave behind.
- They facilitate support networks for families – they are also suffering.
- They educate people about hospice care, so that people donate as well as understand their work.

Supporting those who are mourning

Revised

If you are mourning, it means you are experiencing sadness because of the death of someone. Some people begin to mourn even before the person has died. They have to think of a future without that person, but also help them get their matters in order as well as supporting them. Those mourning may also need support – counselling, kind words, help with doing jobs and legal advice, for example.

How religions help

Revised

- Some religions set up hospices.
- They help the dying by giving them an idea of what will happen after they die – which is good if you have been good! They will give pastoral care – visiting the dying, praying with or for them, helping sort out their affairs.
- They help those who are mourning in the same way, reassuring them about the dying person, being there to listen to them in their grief, perhaps even helping them plan funerals, etc.

Topic basics 4: Euthanasia

What is euthanasia?

Revised

Euthanasia is a compassionate act to help someone die who is terminally ill, has a degenerative disease and is suffering excessively, or is on **life support** with no hope of recovery. With the exception of switching off life support under certain conditions, euthanasia is illegal in the UK. It is punishable under the Suicide Act (1961), and can lead to a sentence of up to fourteen years.

Doctors in the UK swear the Hippocratic Oath, based on the promises made by Hippocrates in ancient Greece, promising to try their best to heal. It also says 'I will give no deadly medicine to anyone if asked, nor suggest such counsel'. In 1516, Thomas More (who was made a saint by the Catholic Church) defended euthanasia as the last treatment option for some patients in his book *Utopia*. Doctors today vary in their attitudes towards it.

Key terms

Euthanasia – mercy killing; a gentle death; helping someone to die who is terminally ill or has a degenerative illness and is suffering; it can be active, passive, voluntary or involuntary

Life support – medical processes, equipment and support to keep a person alive when their own body is not functioning and they are likely to die otherwise

Types of euthanasia

Revised

- **Active euthanasia** is where something is done that leads directly to death, e.g. giving someone a lethal injection.
- **Passive euthanasia** is where support is taken away allowing the illness to kill the person, e.g. switching off life support.
- **Voluntary euthanasia** is where the dying person asks to be helped to die; they know they are terminally ill and do not want to suffer any more.
- **Non-voluntary euthanasia** is where the dying person is unable to ask for euthanasia, but their family sees it as the best option, because the person is on life support and will not recover.

Exam tip

The exam might ask about specific types of euthanasia – so know them all clearly. Attitudes to euthanasia may vary dependent on the type, which makes it easier to write a broader answer with more detail – so better marks.

For and against euthanasia

Revised

For	Against
It is our life, so it should be our right to decide when we have had enough.	Life is given by God, so only God has the right to decide when it ends.
It is an act of compassion when medicine can do no more.	Euthanasia is simply a form of murder.
For some people, life is so wretched they should be able to choose to die.	To allow euthanasia would be to encourage it, because people would abuse it to get their own way, e.g. to claim an inheritance.
There is no point keeping a body alive if there is no hope of recovery.	The person may need to suffer to make up for things they have done.

The life-support issue

Revised

Some patients are on life support, which means that a series of machines is helping them to continue to live. They may be being helped to breathe, or being fed, or their heart may be being helped to keep beating. Doctors will continue this medical treatment while they believe the person might recover. However, in the case of final stage terminal or degenerative illness, they know recovery is not possible. Also if the patient is in PVS (persistent vegetative state), there is no chance of recovery.

If doctors believe that the person will not recover, they will recommend to the family the switching off of the machine, allowing them to die. This is passive euthanasia, but the doctor cannot be prosecuted, because it is really an acknowledgement that the person was already dead.

Exam tip

Questions about whether religious believers agree with life support hinge on the potential for recovery of the patient – that gives you debating room, and broadens your answer.

Religious attitudes to euthanasia

Revised

Most religions are completely against euthanasia as they believe in the **sanctity of life**. They see it as killing someone before God has decided it was their time to die. Many believe God has a plan for each of us, which doesn't include an unnatural end to our life. The worst thing a person can do to another is kill them – it is against the core rules of every religion. Also, for those religions that teach rebirth and/or reincarnation, the suffering being lived through helps to repay bad karma, and so is positive in this way – the suffering will have to be faced in some lifetime. So, both active and voluntary euthanasia would always be seen as wrong in these contexts.

As for passive euthanasia, many religious people think it is wrong to switch off life support unless there is absolutely no chance of recovery. There have been famous cases where the Roman Catholic Church has legally challenged decisions to switch off life support for long-term coma victims. These believers think God will eventually intervene. However, the vast majority of religious believers would see passive euthanasia as acceptable – a necessary evil to end suffering.

Some religious believers see euthanasia as the final medical help a doctor can give, and a gift from God. Groups such as the Dutch Protestant Church will even attend when the person is to be euthanised.

Key term

Sanctity of life – the belief that life is special and/or sacred, because God made it or because of the soul or anatta

Exam tip

Writing about euthanasia, remember to make the point that religious believers within the same religion may have different views.

Buddhism

- We may carry our mothers on one shoulder, and our fathers on the other, and look after them for a hundred years ... we will still be in debt to them.
- Metta and compassion for all sentient beings.
- The First Precept is help, not harm, other sentient beings.
- A primary guiding principle in Buddhism is the relief of suffering.
- In the event a person is definitely going to die ... and prolonging his existence is only going to cause suffering, the termination of his life may be permitted according to Mahayana Buddhist ethics (Dalai Lama).

Sikhism

- It is the greatest sin to quarrel with parents who have given you birth and brought you up (Adi Granth).
- God sends us and we take birth. God calls us back and we die (Guru Granth Sahib).
- All life is sacred and should be respected (Guru Granth Sahib).
- Suffering is part of human life and has a place in God's scheme, so it should be alleviated but not cut short (karma).
- If a Sikh cannot cure or heal a patient, they may not take their life.

Christianity

- Honour your father and mother (Ten Commandments).
- God gives and God takes life (Old Testament).
- Do not kill (Ten Commandments).
- Following Natural Law means that the end of life should be natural, not man-made (Roman Catholic teachings).
- Doctors do not have an overriding obligation to prolong life by all means available (Church of England).

All religions teach:
- stewardship
- sanctity of life
- companionship

Judaism

- Honour your father and mother (Ten Commandments).
- It is forbidden to do anything which shortens a person's life (Talmud).
- G-d gives life, and G-d takes life away (Psalms).
- Do not kill (Ten Commandments).
- One who is in a dying condition is regarded as a living person in all respects (Talmud).

Exam tip

Learn one specific teaching for each aspect of a topic. It gives a stronger answer to be able to say 'Honour your father and mother' than just to use 'Love your neighbour' in the case of attitudes to the elderly, for example.

Islam

- Your Lord orders that you ... be kind to your parents. Say 'Lord bless them, they nurtured, cherished and sustained me in childhood' (Qur'an).
- Neither kill nor destroy yourself (Qur'an).
- No one can die except by Allah's leave, that is a decree with a fixed term (Qur'an).
- Euthanasia is zulm – a wrong-doing against Allah (Shari'ah Law).
- Whoever kills a man ... it shall be as if he had killed all mankind (Qur'an).

Hinduism

- All men come into this world burdened by ancestor debt. Just as our parents looked after us, we must look after them in their old age (Pitri-rin).
- The whole purpose of human existence is to benefit other people through one's life, possessions, thoughts and words (Bhagavata Purana).
- Ahimsa (non-harming) and compassion are basic principles of Hinduism.
- The result of a virtuous action is pure joy; actions done from emotion bring pain and suffering (Bhagavad Gita).
- The one who tries to escape from the trials of this life by taking their own life will suffer even more in the next (Yajur Veda).

Exam practice

What questions on this topic look like:
Religious attitudes to the elderly and death

Check back to pages 11–12 to see the grids examiners use to mark questions worth three or more marks.

This page contains a range of examples of questions that could be on an exam paper for this topic. Practise them all to strengthen your knowledge and technique while revising. Check the website for answers to some of these, with tips.

1 What is meant by quality of life? [1]

2 What is meant by euthanasia? [1]

3 What is a hospice? [1]

4 Explain what is meant by death. [2]

5 Give **two** reasons why some people agree with euthanasia. [2]

6 Give **two** ways in which religious believers can support the elderly. [2]

7 'Old people are no use to society.' What do you think? Explain your opinion. [3]

8 Explain religious attitudes to active euthanasia. [3]

9 Explain religious beliefs about life after death. [3]

10 Explain religious attitudes to caring for the elderly. Refer to beliefs and teachings in your answer. [4]

11 Explain how belief in sanctity of life might affect attitudes to the dying. [4]

12 Explain how believing in life after death might affect how people behave. [4]

13 Explain religious attitudes to euthanasia. You may refer to religious beliefs and teachings in your answer. [5]

14 Explain religious attitudes to the use of life-support machines. [5]

15 Explain how religious believers might help those who are dying. [5]

16 'There is no such thing as life after death.' Do you agree? Give reasons for your answer, showing you have thought about more than one point of view. Refer to religious arguments in your answer. [6]

17 'Religious believers should look after their elderly relatives.' Do you agree? Give reasons for your answer, showing you have thought about more than one point of view. Refer to religious arguments in your answer. [6]

18 'Euthanasia should be available as a medical right.' Do you agree? Give reasons for your answer, showing you have thought about more than one point of view. Refer to religious arguments in your answer. [6]

Online

Exam tip

Did you know that F-grade candidates seem to just spot a word in the question and write about that. This means they often give an answer that fits, but it sometimes means they completely misread the question, e.g. answering 'how' not 'why', or writing why something is legal when they have been asked why it is illegal.

Did you know that C-grade candidates answer most questions in the way the examiner wants, though they might make occasional slips? What they do less well is to judge the exact needs of the question – they miss the key command words, e.g. just listing reasons instead of explaining any of them.

Did you know that A-grade candidates usually answer to show they understood the command words (words that instruct, like 'explain') and the key idea of the question. This means they include the right level of detail, and make the answer fit what the question was looking for. It makes their work very easy to follow and mark.

So, which one are you?

Topic 3 Religious attitudes to drug abuse

Topic basics 1: Mind and body

Religious attitudes to the mind and body ────────── Revised ☐

- Religious traditions teach that human life is valuable (**sanctity of life**).

- The physical **body** is a shell through which the real inner self is expressed.

- The soul (atman) is the real essence of a person.

So ...

Some religious believers think the body is not important and can hinder spiritual development because of physical needs and desires. Some religious believers subject the body to physical suffering to encourage spiritual growth.

But ...

Most religious believers think it is important to care for the body.

They may believe it is on loan from God, or a gift from God, or the means through which they are able to experience God.

Key terms

Sanctity of life – the belief that human life is special, sacred, valuable

Body – the physical make up of a person which can be affected by drugs

Exam tip

This is a really difficult topic. It's a good idea to have two or three examples from the religions you have studied that show this idea. These will help you illustrate and extend your answers.

Religious practices that promote a healthy body and mind ────────── Revised ☐

- Moral codes – encourage a moral life, e.g. honesty, respect for others.

- Community – support arising from being a member of a faith community.

- Lifestyle – encourages care of self, e.g. restrictions on use of drugs and alcohol.

- Discipline – rules and practices that encourage self-discipline.

- Meditation – helps clear and focus the **mind** and achieve a sense of peace.
- Prayer – regular prayer helps believers think about their values and feel supported.
- Confession – helps believers clear their conscience by repenting wrong-doing (sins).

What are drugs?

Revised

Drugs are substances that affect the body and mind in some way. This means that religious people are influenced by their beliefs and teachings when deciding about the use of drugs. Attitudes to using drugs vary depending on whether the drugs are legal or illegal.

> **Key term**
>
> **Mind** – the conscious part of the brain that can be affected by drug use

Medically prescribed drugs

Revised

Medically prescribed drugs are drugs that are legal to use. They include drugs prescribed by a doctor and those that can be bought from the chemist. All religions permit the use of these drugs because they are taken to help someone get well again or to relieve suffering and pain.

> **Key term**
>
> **Medically prescribed drugs** – drugs prescribed by a doctor as part of medical treatment

Common mistakes

Revised

Candidates sometimes make the mistake of saying that religious believers are totally against using drugs and make their answer even worse by going on to say that they think this is wrong because you should be allowed to take medicines! Remember: NO religion says it is wrong to use medically prescribed drugs.

Topic basics 2: Legal drugs

Legal drugs and taxation

Revised

Legal drugs include tobacco and alcohol. In the UK these drugs are allowed by law and can be bought by anyone over the age of eighteen. The government taxes these drugs. This means that when someone buys a tobacco or alcohol product, some of the money paid will go to the government.

Why tax legal drugs?

- To discourage people from using them.
- The drugs can lead to health problems increasing the costs of health care, so discouraging their use will save money in the long term.
- To raise money for the government to spend on public services, e.g. health care.
- They are luxury items so people should pay taxes on them if they have money to spend on them in the first place.
- Taxes could be used to fund medical research and the treatment of addicts.

> **Key terms**
>
> **Legal drugs** – drugs that can be purchased legally; some have age restrictions
>
> **Taxation** – a legal levy by government taking a portion of the money from the sale of goods, e.g. alcohol and tobacco products

> **Exam tip**
>
> Learn some advantages and disadvantages of taxing legal drugs. Make sure you can say why religious believers would agree and/or disagree with raising money through the **taxation** of legal drugs.

Religious attitudes to legal drugs

Revised

Religious believers are guided by their beliefs and practices. Religions have different attitudes to the use of legal drugs. Some believers think it is okay to use these drugs in moderation because their teachings do not forbid them and may even use them (e.g. wine) in some of their religious celebrations. Other believers think that they should not use any drug that is damaging to their body and mind. They may even have specific teachings that forbid the use of these drugs.

Tobacco

Revised

The drug in tobacco is nicotine. It is usually smoked in cigarettes but is also found in cigars, chewing tobacco and 'snuff'. Users get addicted to nicotine very quickly and the habit can be very difficult to break because as well as the physical side effects of quitting, users also associate smoking with relaxation.

Exam tip

'Legal drugs' includes medicines, tobacco, alcohol and caffeine. In any question, refer to all to increase the breadth of your answer and hence increase your marks.

Impact of tobacco use

● Cost – high taxation makes smoking very expensive.
● Health – smoking has been proven to shorten life span, cause serious heart and lung diseases and breathing problems.
● Environment – smoke pollutes the environment with its smell and waste products; it also affects the health of others through passive smoking.

Many religious believers do not use tobacco because it is damaging to the body.

Alcohol

Revised

Most adults in the UK use alcohol. Many religious believers see nothing wrong with the use of alcohol in moderation. Alcohol abuse is wrong because of the long-term damaging effects on the body, the family and society.

Exam tip

It is good to learn the teachings of two specific religions on alcohol use: one that allows the use of alcohol and one that forbids it.

Caffeine

Revised

Caffeine is a stimulant mostly consumed in drinks such as coffee, tea and energy drinks, etc. Most religions do not forbid its use, but individual believers may choose not to use caffeine because of its effects.

Topic basics 3: Illegal drugs

How are illegal drugs classified?
Revised

Illegal drugs are those that are considered to be particularly harmful. The Misuse of Drugs Act (1979) **classifies drugs** into three classes as shown below. It is illegal to possess, use or sell these drugs and offenders can be prosecuted and punished.

Drug class	Examples	Maximum prison sentence
Class A (most harmful)	Heroin, cocaine, ecstasy, crack, crystal-meth	Possession: 7 years / fine Selling: life imprisonment
Class B	Cannabis, amphetamines (speed) Methylphenidate (Ritalin)	Possession: 5 years / fine Selling: 14 years
Class C (least harmful)	Steroids, tranquillisers, magic mushrooms	Possession: 2 years / fine Selling: 14 years

Key terms

Illegal drugs – any drugs that are illegal to possess, sell or use, listed in the classification of drugs

Classification of drugs – the legal system which classifies illegal drugs into categories A, B, C according to the level of harm they do and how addictive they are

The law and drugs
Revised

Illegal drugs are classified by the government:

● because they are the most harmful drugs
● to try to prevent their use
● to warn people of the dangers of using these drugs
● to punish dealers and users fairly
● because they cause harm to families and society
● because they are highly addictive.

The debate about legalising all drugs:

● Legal drugs are just as harmful in the long term; smoking and alcohol abuse kills people.
● Making drugs illegal encourages people to use them (thrill factor).
● Legalising Class A, B and C drugs would reduce crime, allow freedom of choice, control the production and supply of these drugs and raise money through taxation.
● It would prevent 'drug lords' from amassing wealth and power.
● Drugs like cannabis are so widely used it is impossible to police fairly.

Common mistakes

Some candidates have confused knowledge, especially about cannabis. It is NOT legal to possess cannabis (it is a Class B drug). It is NOT a cure for some illnesses (it is a relaxant, which diverts awareness from pain). It is NOT prescribed in a form that is smoked.

Revised

Exam tip

Make sure you are able to give reasons for and against the legal status of different drugs including tobacco, alcohol and cannabis.

Religious attitudes to illegal drugs
Revised

All religious traditions teach that it is wrong to use illegal drugs because:

● they harm the body (gift of God)
● they can result in early death (sanctity of life)
● they destroy families and harm society (golden rule)
● they are illegal (obey societies rules).

N.B. A small minority of believers in some religious traditions do use cannabis-like plants to induce a meditative state as part of their religious practice.

Exam tip

When asked to explain religious attitudes, you should use religious teachings and beliefs to illustrate why religious believers have these attitudes.

Topic basics 4: Drug use and addiction

The risks of drug use

Revised

- Health – all drugs affect the body and mind in the short and long term.
- Financial – addiction is costly; all drugs cost money and a 'habit' can be very expensive.
- Uncertainty – illegal drugs are not controlled; users could be exposed to other poisons mixed with the drug.
- Criminal – if caught, illegal drug users risk getting a criminal record, heavy fines, imprisonment, etc.

Consequences of drug use

Revised

- Physical – addiction, damage to health, shortened life expectancy, death.
- Mental – addiction, mental health issues such as irrational thinking, psychosis and depression.
- Social – family breakdown, inability to work, crime, cost of health services and help for addicts.
- **Recreational** – drugs used for fun, socialising, etc. can become addictive and lead to use of harder drugs.

Exam tip

Read questions carefully. If you are asked to give two social consequences of drug use, you will not be credited if you say they damage your health and lead to addiction as these are physical consequences, not social.

Key term

Recreational drug – any drug used for recreational and social purposes, e.g. for fun

Helping addicts

Revised

Drug use can lead to addiction. People can be caught up in a vicious circle of addiction which makes it impossible for them to live their life happily and safely. Breaking the addiction often needs specialist advice and support.

- **Rehabilitation** centres – these are specialist units run by health care professionals. They are often residential and use a range of therapies, treatments and counselling to help addicts rebuild their lives.
- Drug therapies – addicts can experience severe physical and mental suffering when they stop using a drug. Replacement drug therapies like nicotine patches ease these withdrawal symptoms.
- Counselling – support and guidance by trained experts can help addicts understand why they have turned to drug use. By dealing with the underlying causes of drug taking, they can be helped to quit.
- Voluntary self-help – organisations like Alcoholics Anonymous (AA) provide a forum for addicts to share their experiences with others who are in the same situation, and support each other in quitting.
- Charitable organisations – these are religious and secular groups that work with addicts who have nowhere else to turn for help.

Key term

Rehabilitation – the process by which addicts are helped to overcome addiction

Exam tip

Make sure you know about the work of an organisation that helps addicts. You can use this as an example to explain how addicts can be rehabilitated.

Religious attitudes to addiction

Revised

Religious teachings encourage believers to care for their body and mind. Following the teachings would mean that believers should not become addicted to drug use. When someone is addicted, even if they are not religious, believers think that all people should be treated equally and with compassion. This means that religious teachings encourage believers to help and support addicts in overcoming their addictions.

Each religion has teachings that encourage believers to help addicts, as shown below.

Religions	Teachings
Buddhism	• Metta – 'loving kindness' should be shown to all. • Skilful keeping of the precept to not harm; use it to help others.
Christianity	• Love your neighbour. • Do unto others as you would have done to you.
Hinduism	• Atman is within all. • The Bhagavad Gita states that to reach liberation you should work for others.
Islam	• Allah loves the fair-minded. • Make not your own hands contribute to your destruction. • He who saves the life of one man, it is as if he saves all of humanity.
Judaism	• Practise justice, love and kindness to all. • God created all in His image.
Sikhism	• Using the same mud the creator has created many shapes in many ways. • Those who love God, love everyone.

Religious teachings on religious attitudes to drug abuse: good teachings to learn

Sikhism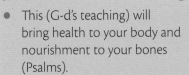

- The pain of selfishness is gone. I have found peace, my body has become healthy (Guru Granth Sahib).
- The Khalsa abided by the Kurahits (prohibitions) which forbid use of alcohol and tobacco.
- Drinking wine, his intelligence departs and madness enters his mind (Guru Amar Das).
- Rahit Maryada forbids the use of all intoxicants that affect the mind.
- Meditation on God's name requires Sikhs to have a clear mind.

Buddhism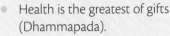

- Health is the greatest of gifts (Dhammapada).
- To abstain from taking intoxicants (Fifth Precept).
- Right Meditation (eighth step of the Eightfold Path, requires clear mind).
- Desire causes attachment (e.g. addiction); it can be overcome in the Buddhist lifestyle.
- Addicts should be treated with metta (loving kindness, compassion).

Christianity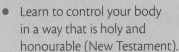

- Learn to control your body in a way that is holy and honourable (New Testament).
- The body is a temple of the Holy Spirit (New Testament).
- Do not get drunk on wine, it leads to sinfulness, instead be filled with the Holy Spirit. (New Testament).
- The use of drugs inflicts grave damage on human health; the use of them except on therapeutic grounds is a grave sin (Roman Catholic Church).
- Drink a little wine to aid your digestion (New Testament).

All religions teach:
- sanctity of life
- justice and social harmony
- repentance and forgiveness

Judaism

- This (G-d's teaching) will bring health to your body and nourishment to your bones (Psalms).
- Wine is a mocker and beer a brawler, whoever is led astray by them is not wise (Proverbs).
- Blessed are you, Lord our G-d, King of the universe, who creates the fruit of the wine (Jewish blessing made over wine for ceremonies).
- During Purim an ancient teaching advises to drink until tipsy and unsure of blessing Mordechai or cursing Haman.
- The body is on loan until the day of resurrection, it should not be harmed.

Islam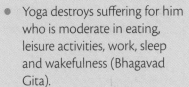

- We give through this Qur'an all that gives health and is a grace to those who believe (Qur'an).
- Alcohol is the mother of all evil (Hadith).
- Alcohol and gambling are an abomination of Satan's work (Qur'an).
- Shari'ah law imposes strict penalties for the use and possession of illegal drugs.
- The body is a gift of Allah that should be cared for and not abused.

Hinduism

- Yoga destroys suffering for him who is moderate in eating, leisure activities, work, sleep and wakefulness (Bhagavad Gita).
- Drink and drugs taxation is degrading, it should be returned tenfold in the form of necessary services (Mohandas Gandhi).
- Sadhu (holy men) use natural plant substances as part of heightened meditation.
- Hinduism teaches that the use of alcohol and drugs is a matter of conscience.
- O God, you alone create the medicines that heal us (Rig Veda).

Exam tip

Ideas like 'sanctity of life', 'God created us', and 'need to be able to focus on God in worship' can be used in this topic for all its aspects – mind, body, legal and illegal drugs, and addicts. So use them, but make sure you say how they fit the aspect and don't just write them for the examiner to do it for you.

Exam practice

What questions on this topic look like:
Religious attitudes to drug abuse

Check back to pages 11–12 to see the grids examiners use to mark questions worth three or more marks.

This page contains a range of examples of questions that could be on an exam paper for this topic. Practise them all to strengthen your knowledge and technique while revising. Check the website for answers to some of these, with tips.

1   Name a legal drug. [1]

2   Give **one** reason why religious believers would agree with taxation on legal drugs. [1]

3   What is meant by the term recreational drug? [1]

4   Give **two** reasons why some people use illegal drugs. [2]

5   Explain briefly what is meant by the classification of drugs. [2]

6   Explain briefly **one** reason why people might use illegal drugs. [2]

7   Explain why religious believers disagree with drink driving. [3]

8   Explain why many religious believers would support the rehabilitation of drug addicts. [3]

9   'Religious believers should only use drugs that have been prescribed.' What do you think? Explain your opinion. [3]

10 Explain **two** reasons why religious believers think it is wrong to use illegal drugs. [4]

11 Explain religious attitudes to the care of the body and mind. [4]

12 Describe ways in which religious believers could help those suffering from addiction. [4]

13 Explain religious attitudes towards the use of alcohol. Refer to beliefs and teachings in your answer. [5]

14 Explain religious teachings about the use of tobacco. [5]

15 Explain why religious believers are opposed to the use of illegal drugs. [5]

16 'People should not be forbidden from using illegal drugs if they want to.' Do you agree? Give reasons for your answer, showing you have thought about more than one point of view. Refer to religious arguments in your answer. [6]

17 'Alcohol should be made illegal in the UK.' Do you agree? Give reasons for your answer, showing you have thought about more than one point of view. Refer to religious arguments in your answer. [6]

18 'Religious believers should support the taxation of legal drugs.' Do you agree? Give reasons for your answer, showing you have thought about more than one point of view. Refer to religious arguments in your answer. [6]

Online

Exam tip

Did you know that F-grade candidates often just give an opinion in evaluative questions. It is often not even related to the statement, so doesn't give anything worthy of credit, or beyond minimal credit. If this is you, train yourself to give a reason to agree and disagree.

Did you know that C-grade candidates often describe attitudes in evaluative questions, so, for example, the question might be about whether a certain drug should be legalised, but they just write about what religions think about drugs. For evaluative questions, you have to evaluate – give arguments for and against the statement. If this is you – practise.

Did you know that A-grade candidates do evaluate both sides in evaluative questions. They give arguments to agree and disagree with the statement, and explain them. Where they mention religious believers, they don't just write about attitudes, they explain what a religious believer's perspective might be on that statement.

So, which one are you?

Topic 4 Religious attitudes to crime and punishment

Key knowledge

- The concepts of right and wrong, justice, conscience.
- Why people commit crime.
- Why we punish (aims of punishment).
- Types of punishment, custodial and non-custodial.
- Religious attitudes to:
  - law
  - punishment
  - treatment of offenders
  - capital punishment.
- Why people agree or disagree with capital punishment.

Topic basics 1: Crime and the causes of crime

Different types of crime
Revised

There are a number of different types of **crime**:

- **Crimes against a person** – these include murder, rape, mugging, assault and slander.
- **Crimes against property** – these include vandalism, theft, trespassing, arson and shop lifting.
- **Crimes against the state** – terrorism, bribery of officials, tax evasion, motoring offences and breaking byelaws.

Exam tip

Ensure you are able to give specific examples of crimes that fit in each of these categories.

Key terms

Crime – an offence that breaks the law and is punishable through the law

Crime against a person – a crime that physically and/or mentally harms another person

Crime against property – a crime that damages someone else's property

Crime against the state – a crime that undermines the authority of the government or state

Why do people commit crimes?
Revised

There are many reasons why some people choose to break the **law**. Usually offenders have committed their crimes for more than one reason. The reasons fit broadly into four categories:

Key term

Law – the rules of society put in place by government

1 Social reasons – peer pressure such as membership of a gang or the need to fit in; some may even disagree with a law and so break it deliberately.

2 Environmental reasons – poverty, upbringing and where people live can all influence some people to commit crimes.

3 Psychological reasons – human nature such as being greedy, jealous or aggressive or more deep-seated psychological problems such as sociopaths and kleptomaniacs.

4 Drug addiction – crime figures show that drug addiction and the illegal production, trafficking and sale of drugs is the highest single cause of crime. The use of legal drugs like alcohol also contributes to crime figures with ordinarily law-abiding people committing crimes as a consequence of impaired judgement.

> **Exam tip**
>
> If asked to explain why people commit crimes, it is a good idea to include examples of the types of crime they might commit because of this reason. For example, jealousy can make some people steal or destroy other people's belongings.

Religious offences
Revised

Religious offences can be when a religious believer fails to follow the moral codes of their religion. These are called sins. Sins are not always crimes, because they do not break society's laws, but sometimes they can be both sins and crimes.

Religious offences can also be understood as crimes against religion and include attacks on religious believers as a consequence of religious prejudice (hate crimes), damaging holy buildings, theft of religious artefacts, etc.

> **Key term**
>
> **Religious offence** – a crime against religion or when a religious believer breaks their religious rules (a sin)

Common mistakes
Revised

Candidates who are unsure of the distinction between sins and crimes can find it difficult to explain the term 'religious offence'. Make sure that you know examples of actions that are sins only; and actions that are sins as well as crimes. Use these to make your answers clear.

Topic basics 2: Aims of punishment

The aims of punishment
Revised

The **aims of punishment** are:

- **deterrence** – to put people off committing crimes
- **protection** – to keep the public safe from dangerous **criminals**
- **reformation** – to change a criminal's behaviour for the good
- **reparation** – to make up for a crime committed
- **retribution** – to get revenge on a criminal
- **vindication** – to ensure that the law is respected.

> **Key terms**
>
> **Aims of punishment** – the reasons why criminals are punished for breaking the law: deterrence, protection, reformation, reparation, retribution and vindication
>
> **Criminal** – a person who breaks the law
>
> **Punishment** – consequence of being found guilty of a crime

> **Exam tip**
>
> The aims of punishment will always be on the exam paper. Even if there are no questions using these words, at least one of the questions will be asked in such a way that you can use this information. For example, 'Explain religious attitudes to the treatment of young offenders.'
> A good way to answer this is to explain why religious believers would consider reformation, reparation and vindication the most important aims in sentencing a young offender.

Strengths and weaknesses of the different aims of punishment

Revised

Aim of punishment	Strengths	Weaknesses
Deterrence	• Puts people off reoffending • Stops people committing a crime	• Many offenders do not think about the consequences of their action • People who decide to commit a crime do not think they will get caught
Protection	• Keep people safe from dangerous offenders • Prevent property from being damaged	• **Parole** and **early release** mean some dangerous offenders are let out • All crimes hurt someone, you can't lock up every criminal
Reformation	• Helps offenders understand the effects of their crime • Helps offenders live an honest lifestyle	• Some people see this as 'soft sentencing' • Criminals get 'rewarded' for their crime with training programmes, support services, etc.
Reparation	• Offenders can help make up for what they have done • Victims receive some compensation for their loss	• Things like community service are not seen as proper punishments • Money does not make up for the physical and emotional harm the victim has to live with
Retribution	• Offenders get what they deserve for their crimes • Society takes revenge on behalf of the victim, makes things even	• Severe sentences have been imposed on innocent people • No punishment can ever make up for the harm done to many victims
Vindication	• The law works because people are punished for breaking it • People respect the law	• Some laws are trivial and out of date • Some offenders really need help, not punishment

Key terms

Parole – releasing a prisoner early from prison because they have behaved well and accepted responsibility for their crimes

Early release – criminals who have not completed their prison sentence are let out early without meeting the requirements for parole

Exam tip

Use the strengths and weaknesses of the different aims of punishment when asked to evaluate the most important aims of punishment.

Law and order

Revised

To maintain law and **order** in society it is important that when people do wrong they do not get away with it. Offenders are punished to bring about **justice**. This means that victims of crime can be reassured that they are valued in society and that everything is being done to ensure that what happened to them is not repeated. It also means that offenders are treated fairly and that their punishment fits their crime.

Key terms

Order – the state of peace and harmony in society when the law is followed

Justice – bringing about fairness, putting right a wrong action

Religious attitudes to law and order

All religions teach the **importance of respecting the law** and **following rules** of society. However, they do also encourage believers to **challenge unjust laws** and to **come to the defence** of those who are persecuted or unfairly treated. Religious teachings support the idea that **offenders need to be punished** suitably if they commit crimes. In some cases they do support severe penalties, but this is to achieve **justice and reparation NOT for retribution** as the main aim.

All religions encourage offenders to **take responsibility for their actions**. This means there is a **duty to punish** offenders, but also to help them **admit to and repent for** their actions. Religious teachings encourage **forgiveness**, because all people are capable of making mistakes and have the **ability to change**. Many religious believers would therefore see **reformation as the most important aim** of punishment.

Common mistakes

Some candidates say that because religions teach forgiveness they do not agree with punishing criminals. This is NOT accurate. Religions teach that offenders can be forgiven, but they must first repent for their crime. Even so, they must also be punished as this is part of achieving justice in society.

Revised ☐

Key terms

Responsibility – having a duty to care for someone or something

Duty – a moral or legal obligation to do the right thing

Forgiveness – showing mercy, compassion; accepting someone even if they have done wrong

Exam tip

The words and phrases in bold are the key ideas for you to learn. If you use these correctly in your answers to exam questions, you will improve your answers.

Religion and human nature

Revised ☐

Religious attitudes to crime and punishment are influenced by the teachings and beliefs about people and human nature. Use these ideas to illustrate answers to questions about religious attitudes on this topic.

- Human life is valuable.
- All people have a **conscience**.
- All people are capable of right and wrong actions.

- People are sometimes driven by selfish needs.
- People need moral codes to guide them in making decisions.

Key term

Conscience – the inner voice that tells a person they are doing right or wrong

Exam tip

Make sure you know the main teachings in the moral codes of the religions you are studying, e.g. the Ten Commandments (Christianity and Judaism), Rahit Maryada (Sikhism). Make sure you understand how these teachings influence attitudes to the issues in this topic.

Topic basics 3: Punishments and attitudes to offenders

Different types of punishment

Revised ☐

There are a number of different types of punishment:

- **Community service** – punishment requiring a person to do unpaid work in the community.
- **Fines** – the requirement of a criminal to pay a sum of money as a punishment.
- **Imprisonment** – locking someone up in a prison for crimes committed.
- **Prison** – government institution used to lock up some convicted criminals.

- **Probation** – an alternative to prison where offenders are monitored by a probation officer to ensure they are not offending any more.
- **Tagging** – the use of an electronic monitoring device to track the movements of an offender who has been allowed to return into the community.

How are offenders punished?

In the UK a diverse range of punishments are used. These are broadly divided into two categories: custodial sentences (which lock people up) and non-custodial sentences (alternatives to prison).

	Pro	Con
Prisons	• Protects the public • Punishes the offender • Offenders can learn how to behave responsibly in society	• Expensive form of punishment • Puts like-minded people together • Can encourage more crime • Prisons are too overcrowded to effectively reform criminals
High-security psychiatric hospitals	• Protect the public from dangerous offenders • Provide proper care for criminals who are mentally ill • Removes the risk of reoffending since offenders cannot be released unless they are well	• Very expensive • Not seen as a punishment • If released the person needs to continue being treated or they may reoffend
Young Offender Institutions	• Focus on education and training • Teach young people skills and responsibility • Promote self-discipline	• Serious crimes not suitably punished • No female youth offender institutes so they go to special units attached to women's prisons • Can be a long way from family

Alternatives to prison

- ASBO
- Community service
- Curfew
- Electronic tagging
- Fines
- Probation
- Restorative justice
- Corporal punishment

Advantages	Disadvantages
• Costs less than imprisonment • Not all crimes deserve or need the offender to be locked up • Criminal pays back to society in a positive way • Criminals' freedom is curtailed • Offenders learn the value of freedom • Monitors offenders' behaviour • Can be quickly administered	• They don't always work • They are sometimes considered as soft sentencing • Some offenders may see it as a 'badge of honour' • The offender turns to crime to pay fines • Corporal punishment can leave offenders disabled for life

Religious attitudes to young offenders

When people under the age of eighteen commit crimes they are labelled as **young offenders**. Society and religious traditions generally believe that, because of their age, these offenders should be treated differently. When sentencing them emphasis is placed on restorative justice and reforming them. Religions teach that young people should be guided and supported; they should be taught how to live a moral life. Punishment for correction is allowed, but it should be proportional and promote repentance, not be administered as retribution.

Common mistakes

When asked to explain religious attitudes to young offenders, candidates sometimes write about attitudes to offenders generally. It is important to focus your answer on the term 'young offender' and recognise that religious teachings do not promote imprisonment and severe physical punishment of young offenders.

Topic basics 4: Capital punishment

The debate about the death penalty

Capital punishment (also known as the death penalty) is the sentence of death imposed on a criminal by the state. The death penalty is usually reserved for the most serious crimes, such as murder, rape, terrorism and drug offences. Methods of execution include lethal injection, hanging, firing squad, electrocution, beheading and stoning. More than half of countries worldwide have abolished the death penalty. In the UK capital punishment was abolished in 1969. Parliament has repeatedly voted against its reintroduction in the UK.

Arguments for the death penalty

- Retribution is served by 'life for a life'.
- Deterrence against crimes such as terrorism and murder.
- Victims and families receive justice.
- Life sentences do not mean life any more.
- Natural law, life sentence has been used for centuries.
- Protection: dangerous criminals will never reoffend.

Arguments against the death penalty

- Retribution is inhumane; two wrongs do not make a right.
- Mistakes are made; innocent people have been executed.
- Executing terrorists makes them martyrs.
- Most murders are spontaneous, therefore it is not a deterrent.
- It is inhumane and degrading to imprison someone for years and then execute them.
- Killing the offender does not lessen the pain felt by victims and their families.

Key term

Capital punishment – the death penalty, legal execution of a criminal for the crime they were found guilty of committing

Common mistakes

Some candidates when asked about capital punishment insist on also writing about corporal punishment (physical torture such as hand severing and flogging). You will not be credited for writing about corporal punishment, so don't waste time and make your answer look confused by including information that is not about the death penalty.

Revised

Exam tip

If asked about religious attitudes to the death penalty, remember that religious people's opinions are often the same as those of non-religious people. Religious believers therefore have varying attitudes to the death penalty. What makes their attitudes 'religious' is that they have been formed with the influence of their religious beliefs and teachings.

Religious attitudes to the death penalty
Revised

For many religious believers this, like many other moral issues, is a matter of conscience. In most religious teachings it is possible to find instructions both for and against using the death penalty. In forming their opinion, religious people will be guided by their understanding of the religious teachings. Their attitudes may also be formed by the secular society in which they live.

Common mistakes
Revised

Candidates who have studied Christianity often place too much emphasis in their answers on the Old Testament teaching of a 'life for a life'. This is a weak answer when considering Christian attitudes. Most Christians consider Jesus' teaching on forgiveness to have replaced this and so are often very opposed to the use of the death penalty.

Religious action on crime and punishment

Revised ☐

Many religious groups support the equal and just treatment of all people, including offenders. This means that they are active in campaigning for the abolition of the death penalty. They may also work to improve prison standards and the treatment and provision of services for offenders, their families and victims of crime.

Religious teachings on religious attitudes to crime and punishment: good teachings to learn

Revised ☐

Buddhism

- Evil actions are caused by the Three Poisons – greed, anger, ignorance.
- Karuna is the practice of showing compassion for all.
- The story of Milarepa illustrates that all people can change for the better.
- Law of karma – sum total of good and bad actions.
- Abstain from taking what is not freely given (Second Precept).

Sikhism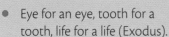

- He who associates with evil doers is destroyed (Guru Granth Sahib).
- Do not strike those who hit you, kiss their feet and return home (Guru Granth Sahib).
- Recognise the Lord's Light (spirit) is within all (Guru Granth Sahib).
- Kirat Karna involves supporting your needs through honest work.
- Kirpan reminds Sikhs to follow the path of justice and fight for truth.

Christianity

- If your brother sins, rebuke him, if he repents forgive him (New Testament).
- Forgive your brother seventy times seven (Jesus) – (Christians should always be prepared to forgive).
- Parable of the Prodigal Son teaches to rejoice and forgive when a sinner repents.
- Forgive us our trespasses as we forgive those who trespass against us (Lord's Prayer).
- Submit to the authorities, who serve at God's will (St Paul).

All religions teach:
- sanctity of life
- justice and social harmony
- repentance and forgiveness

Judaism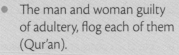

- Eye for an eye, tooth for a tooth, life for a life (Exodus).
- Justice brings joy to the righteous and terror to wrongdoers (Proverbs).
- The Lord does not enjoy seeing sinners die, he would rather they stop sinning and live (Ezekiel).
- Spare the rod and spoil the child (Proverbs).
- Yom Kippur (Day of Atonement) – all Jews confess and make atonement for their sins.

Islam

- The man and woman guilty of adultery, flog each of them (Qur'an).
- As to the thief, cut off their hand, a punishment by way of example (Qur'an).
- If anyone is killed unjustly, we have granted the right of retribution to their heir (Qur'an).
- We ordained for them, life for life (Qur'an).
- Diya (blood money) can be accepted as reparation by the victim.

Hinduism

- Murdering a Brahmin is the most serious of crimes (Laws of Manu).
- If a man sins, in his next rebirth he will be of an inanimate thing, or a beast, or a lower caste (Laws of Manu).
- An eye for an eye and the whole world would be blind (Gandhi).
- When a person claims to be non-violent … he will put up with all the injury given to him by a wrongdoer (Gandhi).
- Karma – all evil actions result in bad karma that lead to negative rebirth.

Exam practice

What questions on this topic look like:
Religious attitudes to crime and punishment

Check back to pages 11–12 to see the grids examiners use to mark questions worth three or more marks.

This page contains a range of examples of questions that could be on an exam paper for this topic. Practise them all to strengthen your knowledge and technique while revising. Check the website for answers to some of these, with tips.

1 Give the meaning of the word crime. [1]

2 What is meant by the term duty? [1]

3 Give an example of a religious offence. [1]

4 Explain briefly **two** reasons why religious believers think that crimes against a person are wrong. [2]

5 Give **two** causes of crime. [2]

6 Explain briefly why it is important for society to punish criminals. [2]

7 Explain why many religious believers agree with the use of community service as a punishment for young offenders. [3]

8 'Religious believers should always do what their conscience tells them.' What do you think? Explain your opinion. [3]

9 'Religious teachings show that reformation is the most important aim of punishment.' What do you think? Explain your opinion. [3]

10 Explain why many religious believers would consider crimes against a person to be worse than crimes against property. [4]

11 Explain religious teachings and beliefs about religious offences. [4]

12 Explain different religious attitudes to parole and early release of prisoners. [4]

13 Explain religious attitudes to the forgiveness of criminals. Refer to beliefs and teachings in your answer. [5]

14 Explain religious attitudes to punishing criminals using alternative ways to prison. [5]

15 Explain religious attitudes to capital punishment (the death penalty). [5]

16 'Young offenders should be helped, not punished.' Do you agree? Give reasons for your answer, showing that you have thought about more than one point of view. Refer to religious arguments in your answer. [6]

17 'Reformation of offenders is more important than retribution.' Do you agree? Give reasons for your answer, showing that you have thought about more than one point of view. Refer to religious arguments in your answer. [6]

18 'Religious people should never commit crimes.' Do you agree? Give reasons for your answer, showing that you have thought about more than one point of view. Refer to religious arguments in your answer. [6]

Online

Exam tip

Did you know that F grade candidates often get the command words wrong? These are the instructions like 'explain' or 'describe', as well as words like 'why' and 'how'. They sometimes ignore the command words and just write about the focus of the question. They often answer a different command – 'why' rather than 'how' for example. They often simply don't understand what they are being asked for. More practise helps resolve this.

Did you know that C grade candidates usually answer the question as commanded, but will mix the words up, and will be less focussed at times on the command – describing rather than explaining for example. Practise makes you understand how the exam is written, and helps you get it right in the exam itself.

Did you know that A grade candidates usually nail the questions? They write their answers precisely to the command words. They use the commands to structure their answers, and avoid writing irrelevant material, and their answers then focus on exactly what the question wants – which means they get the best marks.

So, which are you?

Topic 5 Religious attitudes to rich and poor in British society

Key knowledge

- Why people are rich or poor in the UK.
- Why people do or don't gamble.
- Why some people are homeless.
- How individuals and the government can help the poor.
- Religious attitudes to:
  - the poor in the UK
  - gambling
  - earning money
  - **personal wealth** and its use.

Key term

Personal wealth – the money or valuables that a person has for themselves

Topic basics 1: Poverty in British society

Causes of poverty in Britain

Revised ▢

In Britain we have rich people and poor people but we tend to think Britain is a fairly wealthy country, with support for those who need it.

Poverty is **complex** and a **difficult** issue to solve. Many problems are **interconnected** and sometimes people have little **compassion** for the poor in Britain because we assume it's their **fault** and they are to blame for their own **actions** or **inaction**. Some of this might be true so we use phrases like: 'Well if they hadn't done …', 'It's their own fault because …', 'It's their choice to be …'.

However, the poor in developing countries tend to be seen as innocent victims, poor through no fault of their own. For the exam, remember that wherever the blame lies we have a **responsibility as individuals** to help and as religious believers to help **rather than to judge**.

See the link

Here are some ways in which issues of poverty connect:

- Young people born into poverty – poor home life, parents do not work, both parents not at home, miss school to help out, falls behind, truancy, no qualifications, no college, no job, relies on benefits.
- Attitudes – apathy, laziness, skived school, wrong crowd, crime, drugs, prison, unemployed.
- Situations – business owner, recession, poor investments, bankrupt, loses family and home, no income.
- Illness – good job, heart attack, too ill to work, fear it could happen again, no support.

Key terms

Poverty – lack of wealth to the extent that life is difficult not having even the basic needs of life

Compassion – loving kindness; a desire to help because it is the right thing to do

Exam tip

The words and phrases in bold should help you learn this information.

Exam tip

Make sure answers are focused on issues in Britain. One-mark and two-mark questions often ask you to name the causes. Common mistakes seen are answers based on developing countries (and that is Topic 6).

Exam tip

For three-mark questions asking you to explain causes of poverty, better answers are ones that link the problems. Use a brief real-life situation showing how one thing leads to the next.

Homelessness

In the most serious of cases, poverty leads to **homelessness**. In Britain there are currently estimated to be 1 million homeless people. Homeless figures in Britain include:

- people who live on the streets
- people who live rough
- squatters
- people who sleep on other people's floors
- people who live in hostels.

Who are the homeless people?

- The young – some young people have a difficult home life, suffer abuse or are simply not wanted.
- Adults – some adults fall into the wrong lifestyle including contact with drugs and crime.
- People with mental health and behavioural issues.
- Highly trained former armed forces personnel who have seen active service and cannot cope with life outside the military because of their military experiences.

Around 60 per cent of homeless people in Britain are from minority ethnic groups and there is a growing number of women. Think about the fact that many people are forced by situations into being homeless and feel there is no other option available. Many are genuine cases and need our compassion. At the same time some do actually choose to be homeless but this does not make them bad people. Most homeless people would happily have a home and job, but can't get a home without money. The job gives money, but they can't get a job without a fixed address (a home)!

> **Key term**
>
> Homelessness – the state of having no permanent place to live which would be classed as a home

Topic basics 2: Gambling and the National Lottery

Gambling in Britain — Revised

Gambling is very common in the UK and has many different forms. All major events now have 'odds' on their outcome. You can bet on any event that does not have a guaranteed outcome. Traditionally sport was the focus: results of matches, tournaments, boxing matches, racing, etc. Other areas of gambling include casinos (roulette and card games) and bingo halls. Gambling now covers much wider areas, for example in football rather than just betting on a win or score draw, you can now also bet on the first scorer, the number of yellow and red cards given, numbers of corners, which manager will be sacked, etc. It is also about much more than sport – the next prime minister, the sex and name of a royal baby, the X Factor winner, celebs to divorce or marry, the next number one hit – the list goes on forever.

> **Key term**
>
> Gambling – placing money against the chance of something happening in order to win more money

Why do people gamble?

People have always gambled and their reasons for doing so are to win money, for fun, the thrill of winning or to give a game an interest. However, some people have an **addiction** to gambling.

In Britain gambling has become more popular, with people becoming richer and having money to spare. There are serious gamblers and those who just have the occasional bet. Gambling in the last twenty years has created images that appeal to all kinds of people from the housewife to sports supporters to old people, and so on.

The introduction of satellite TV (Sky, Virgin, etc.) means people can gamble at the press of a button and the options open to us are advertised all the time. People can use interactive TV services, the internet and mobile phones. It's easy – you can gamble without having to leave the house! We are offered free bets to get us started and to get us hooked, for example Bet Fair and Skybet.

Key term

Addiction – being psychologically compelled to keep doing something

Exam tip

Look at TV coverage and advertisements about gambling and check for examples of how they encourage people to gamble.

Outcomes of gambling

Positive outcomes

If people gamble and win some money they might, for example buy something new or go on holiday. They also experience the thrill or buzz of winning. (This buzz can encourage them to gamble more often.)

Negative outcomes

If people gamble unsuccessfully they may lose more than they can afford and possibly lose more times than they win. High level gambling results in some people losing everything and getting into debt, and money can become the centre of life causing greed and making them turn to crime in order to survive, for example.

The UK Lottery

The **Lottery** began in 1994 and offered the chance to win big money (multi-million pound wins) by choosing six numbers and a bonus number from numbers between 1 and 49. The way it is organised makes some people think it is not 'really' gambling as tickets can be bought in local shops and supermarkets. It is on BBC TV on Saturday night, which is seen as family viewing time, and the presenters are well-known celebrities. This can be thought of as gambling with a clean image.

Key term

Lottery – the national gambling game in the UK, which aims to create new millionaires each week; a proportion of the profits are used charitably

Advantages

- The chance of winning a lot of money brings hope for life-changing opportunities, e.g. a luxury lifestyle.
- It would solve financial worries and is easy to play.
- Families and charities are helped with the winnings.
- A percentage of the money taken each week goes to charities and good causes in our communities.

Disadvantages

- It's pure luck and not skill or hard work.
- There is little chance of winning the jackpot.
- Often the jackpots are thought to be too much money for one person to win.
- A win can change life for the worse as it takes away normal life.
- Some people cannot afford to buy the ticket and lose more money.

Exam tip

Most questions in the exam will focus on why religious believers should either agree or disagree with gambling or the lottery. Make sure you know at least three reasons on both sides of the argument. Religious believers will use the reasons given here as well as religious teachings to justify gambling or to criticise it.

Religious attitudes to gambling

Buddhism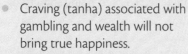

- Craving (tanha) associated with gambling and wealth will not bring true happiness.
- **Wealth** should be earned honestly (Noble Eightfold Path – Right Livelihood).
- We need wealth to meet our needs but no more in case we become attached.

Hinduism

- Uncontrolled pursuit of wealth will result in unhappiness.
- One should accept that which is given to you as your quota.
- Some Hindus accept lottery and gambling in moderation.

Islam

- O you who believe, wine and gambling are filthy tricks of Satan; avoid them so you may pray (Qur'an).
- The profit from gambling is less than the sin gained. It is haram (Hadith).
- Any money gained from gambling cannot be used for good causes in Islam as it is seen as bad money.

Sikhism

- Kirat-Karni means earning one's money by honest means including labour.
- The Guru Granth Sahib says money should not be spent on gambling.
- Two of the five major vices, Lobh (greed) and Moh (worldly attachment), lead to gambling or are fed by gambling.

Christianity

- Gambling goes against the biblical work ethic that associates honest labour with deserved reward. (Gambling is mainly about luck and some people who win do not deserve it.)
- The love of money is the root of all evil (Jesus).
- Some Christians accept fundraising by raffles and some agree the lottery is fine in moderation.
- Some Christians believe that the issue is not about gambling, it is about what you do with the money. If you help your family or **charity** then this justifies the means. Aid money is given but the giver is never asked whether the money has come from acceptable means.

Judaism

- Money should be earned from working – doing G-d's work on earth (Torah).
- The motive for gambling is greed. It is not forbidden but the spiritual consequences are a worry.
- Gambling does take place as part of festivals, e.g. Purim.
- Some Jews believe that playing the lottery is fine in moderation.

Common mistakes

Candidates often do not apply quotations to the topic or they misquote. For example, 'the love of money is the root of all evil' is the correct quotation, not 'money is the root of all evil'.

Key term

Wealth – money, goods or property that someone has; usually in abundance

Charity – support given out of a sense of duty or compassion

Exam tip

Learn three teachings from the religion(s) you have studied.

Exam tip

For each teaching, connect it to the question. For example, the Bible says 'Love of money is the root of all evil' so a Christian would think that gambling is wrong because it is about loving money … Now you have the teaching and the attitude for religious believers today.

Topic basics 3: Wealth in Britain

Sources of wealth in Britain

Revised

Wealth in Britain comes from many sources.

Business and enterprise

- Business – a company that someone runs that they earn money from, and which often employs others.
- Enterprise – a person creates a new product that they might make a fortune from.

Business and enterprise create the majority of wealth in Britain by coming up with products and services that people want to buy, and creating money for owners, employees and shareholders in the process.

Gifts and inheritance

Gifts are usually from someone who is still alive, and may be small or large, and are often money. **Inheritance** comes after the death of someone, and can be very large. It can include possessions as well as property or land, and often money. Inheritance is usually a larger amount of money than a gift.

Earnings and saving

- Earnings – money from a job where people are paid a wage or a salary.
- Savings – money that people keep to one side, perhaps in the bank or invested.

Generally, the better the job the more you earn. Savings are usually taken from what is left after expenses and bills have been paid, and stored away, e.g. in a savings account. Savings are often used in the future when the amount has increased, depending on how much has been saved and the rate of interest paid during the period.

Other ways of making money

Some people gain money through crime, e.g. robbery or drug sales. Some make money through gambling, where no skill is involved, just luck.

> **Exam tip**
>
> Learn the definitions for eight key terms for one-mark questions.
>
> They will often appear as comparison questions so also learn three facts about each key term for a three-mark question.

> **Key term**
>
> **Inheritance** – money, goods or property received from someone because of their death

> **Exam tip**
>
> Think about whether it matters where wealth comes from, whether it is better to earn it or be given it, and the types of jobs that should earn more or less. These are often the focus of three- and six- mark evaluative questions.

Issues connected to sources of wealth

Revised

Minimum wage

The **minimum wage** is the least amount of money an employer can legally pay a worker per hour and it is scaled in four age ranges. The amount is **set by government**. It **protects workers** at the lowest end of the pay scales, who are usually doing unskilled jobs. It protects **employers** from being challenged in court about the wages they pay. **It does not make everyone equal** as skilled jobs often get higher wages than unskilled jobs.

Issues may arise at age 18 or 21 when a worker moves to the next pay level of the minimum wage, thus costing the employer more. This could then lead to the employer employing fewer people.

> **Key term**
>
> **Minimum wage** – the lowest amount a company can legally pay to their workers per hour; it varies depending on age

Excessive (fat-cat) salaries

Excessive 'fat cat' salaries are wages that are viewed as high for the job that is done. Are these wages value for money? Compare a footballer earning £200,000 a week plus bonuses and sponsorship deals to a nurse earning £30,000 a year.

Key term

Excessive (fat cat) salary – a salary paid which is exceptionally high, often including seemingly unnecessary bonuses, often linked to business salaries

Exam tip

Think about these issues in both cases. Does the footballer deserve so much more than the nurse? Have they worked hard enough to get that wage? Why not use the talents and skills they have? Who pays their wages? What is the length of their working life? How much money is too much to earn? Whose opinion matters? These questions all provide areas for evaluation questions.

Topic basics 4: Helping the poor in Britain

Who should care for the poor in Britain?

Revised

1 The government
2 Religious communities
3 Everyone (tax payers and families)
4 Charities
5 The poor themselves

Exam tip

Questions on helping the poor often focus on *how* we help or *whose* responsibility it is to help the poor so prepare some answers. It's easy:

● Learn four answers for *how* we can help.
● Learn three reasons *why* each of the five groups listed above should help.
● Learn three ways each of them can help.

Common mistakes

When the question asks how, many students answer why, which is incorrect. Make sure you read the question carefully.

Revised

How can we help?

Revised

● We can give to charities or the poor directly.
● We can give our time, volunteering help.
● We can raise awareness of poverty issues, e.g. in school assemblies.
● We can campaign for change – protest for more positive government help.

Exam tip

Have some examples to expand these ideas to access the probable four marks available.

Why and how should each group help?

	Why?	How?
Government	• They have the tax money to be able to help • They have access to the organisations that can help all over the country • Their job is to look after the people who elected them	• Benefits system • Back to work training groups • Adult education
Religious communities	• Religious texts tell us to help • Religious figures and leaders helped the poor to set the example • It is a good deed that gets rewarded	• Give money to religious charities • Pray for the poor • Give time and practical help, for example organise food collections
Everyone	• We all have social responsibility to others • We all have compassion to want to help • We would want help if we were in that situation	• Support charities • Give practical help • Campaign for governments to help more
Charities	• They are given money to enable them to help the poor • People will accept help from charities more easily	• Organise practical help like soup kitchens • Advertise and highlight the need for help through the media • Collect money to aid the needy
The poor themselves	• Their poverty may be because of their own actions • They have to want help • Personal pride	• Improve skills or education • Find employment or training • Rehab for drugs issues

Examples of charities that can help

The Salvation Army

This religious group collects money, for example at Christmas in town centres while playing festive music. The group helps rebuild lives by providing rehabilitation, shelters for the homeless and family tracing services among other things. Members offer comfort and support with food parcels, lunch clubs for the elderly and visits to prisoners.

Shelter

This is a non-religious organisation that focuses on the housing problem in Britain. It offers advice for the homeless and assistance for those looking for houses. It campaigns for an increase in social housing as the homeless problem grows. The financial crisis of 2008 made it more difficult for people to buy a house or afford private rents. Shelter fundraises and works politically for change.

Exam tip

The exam might require you to describe the work of a charity working with the poor in Britain, which would usually be a three- or four-mark question. You might be asked about a religious charity or just a charity.

Religious teachings on religious attitudes to rich and poor in British society: good teachings to learn

Revised

Sikhism

- Sikhs tithe (daswandh) – giving ten per cent of their income to the poor.
- Anything earned dishonestly is seen as the 'blood of the poor' – Kirat Karni (honest lifestyle).
- Those who have money have the anxiety of greed, greed being one of the Five Vices.
- For Sikhs, the sign of a good person is that they always seek the welfare of the poor.
- The sign of worship is the service of others – sewa and vand chakna (sharing).

Buddhism

- Riches ruin the foolish – craving for riches causes the foolish man to ruin himself.
- Wealth is acceptable if at the same time it promotes the well-being of society.
- Unskilful thoughts founded in greed keep us attached to this world.
- Dana (charity) is part of merit making and karuna (compassion) wants to see the end of suffering.
- 'If you wish to be happy then care for others' (Dalai Lama).

Christianity

- Be on your guard against all kinds of greed (New Testament).
- No one can serve two masters (New Testament).
- The love of money is the root of all evil (New Testament).
- If anyone has possessions and sees his brother in need how can he love God (Jesus)?
- Whatever you do for others you do for me (Jesus).

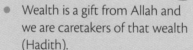

All religions teach:
- justice
- community
- respect
- compassion
- stewardship

Judaism

- Do not weary yourself to become rich (Proverbs).
- He who loves silver cannot be satisfied with silver (Ecclesiastes).
- He who has 100 craves 200.
- Love your neighbour (Leviticus).
- The Talmud says to help the poor cheerfully, compassionately and comfortingly.

Islam

- Wealth is a gift from Allah and we are caretakers of that wealth (Hadith).
- Riches are sweet to those who acquire them by the way, but those who don't seek them out of greed (Qur'an).
- It is not poverty I fear for you, but that you begin to desire the world (Qur'an).
- He who eats and drinks while his brother goes hungry is not one of us (Hadith).
- Giving of zakah and sadaqah is encouraged.

Hinduism

- Uncontrolled pursuit of wealth will result in unhappiness.
- Act in the world as a servant, look after everyone – you are the servant of God (Gandhi).
- Money causes pain when earned, when kept, when lost and when spent.
- To help those in poverty helps one's own rebirth.
- Daya (compassion) and dana (giving to charity).

Common mistakes

Many students make the point that by helping the poor, we make everyone equal. Actually it is most unlikely that we will make everyone equal – we can never give enough – so don't use this argument in your answers.

Also remember that religions do not see any problem with having money – it is how it is earned, and how it is used, that matters. So don't say religions disagree with being rich – they don't.

Revised

Exam tip

Questions are usually about attitudes to money or attitudes about caring for the poor. Make sure you know teachings that apply to each.

Exam tip

It is better to use specific teachings than concepts for the higher grades to be awarded.

What questions on this topic look like:
Religious attitudes to rich and poor in British society

Check back to pages 11–12 to see the grids examiners use to mark questions worth three or more marks.

This page contains a range of examples of questions that could be on an exam paper for this topic. Practise them all to strengthen your knowledge and technique while revising. Check the website for answers to some of these, with tips.

1	What is the Lottery?	[1]
2	Give **one** way someone becomes rich.	[1]
3	What is meant by a fat cat salary?	[1]
4	Explain what is meant by inheritance.	[2]
5	Give **two** reasons why some people may be poor.	[2]
6	Explain what is meant by gambling.	[2]
7	'Religious people should help those affected by poverty.' What do you think? Explain your opinion.	[3]
8	Explain why some religious people disagree with gambling.	[3]
9	Explain why some people live in poverty in the UK.	[3]
10	Explain religious attitudes to the homeless. You may refer to religious beliefs and teachings in your answer.	[4]
11	Explain religious beliefs and teachings about the use of personal wealth.	[4]
12	Explain why some religious people believe it is wrong to play the Lottery.	[4]
13	Explain religious beliefs and teachings about earning money.	[5]
14	Explain how religious people can help the poor in the UK.	[5]
15	Explain religious attitudes to helping the homeless. Refer to beliefs and teachings in your answer.	[5]
16	'Religious believers should help the poor as their first priority.' Do you agree? Give reasons for your answer, showing you have thought about more than one point of view. Refer to religious arguments in your answer.	[6]
17	'It is impossible to end poverty in the UK.' Do you agree? Give reasons for your answer, showing you have thought about more than one point of view. Refer to religious arguments in your answer.	[6]
18	'It does not matter where a person gets their wealth, just how they use it.' Do you agree? Give reasons for your answer, showing you have thought about more than one point of view. Refer to religious arguments in your answer.	[6]

Online

Exam tip

Did you know that F-grade candidates rarely if ever use quotations in their answers? This means that there is nothing concrete in a religious sense in what they are saying, so the examiner can't give good marks.

Did you know that C-grade candidates use religious quotations in some of their answers, and many use them in all their answers? However, they don't show why or how they are directly relevant to the question, and so their answer remains vague. They also use quotations in the wrong place, like trying to make 'Do not kill' fit with this topic, and they misquote.

Did you know that A-grade candidates routinely use religious quotations, and often use quotations from other sources to make their point? They show how they directly link to the question, and very often tell the examiner where the quotation is from, e.g. by saying it is in Leviticus in the Bible, not just writing the quotation with 'Christians say …'. Their work is very clear, and very precise because of the way they use the quotations.

So, which one are you?

Topic 6 Religious attitudes to world poverty

- Understand the concepts of justice, compassion and community.
- Know the causes of world poverty.
- Religious attitudes to:
  - world poverty
  - helping the poor in LEDCs
  - use of personal wealth.
- Know how individuals and groups help the poor in other countries.
- Understand the difference between emergency, short- and long-term aid.
- Understand sustainable development.

Topic basics 1: About worldwide poverty

LEDCs

Revised

The World **Poverty** topic has a focus on areas of the world known collectively as Less Economically Developed Countries (**LEDC**s). Characteristics of such countries are they are **south** of the equator, have **rapidly growing populations**, **climate issues**, are in areas prone to **natural disasters**, have been or are ravaged by **civil war**, have massive **national debt** and are exploited through **world trade** by **richer nations**.

Issues here are simply about survival. There is no blame attached to the poverty these people suffer – it is unfortunate rather than them being to blame. This view obviously affects our attitudes towards them, as we are more compassionate and willing to help.

- LEDCs are mainly in Asia, Africa and South America.
- Forty-nine countries are classed as Less Economically Developed.
- Within this classification there are some '**Least Developed**' countries with **extreme** poverty with all the characteristics above, such as Ethiopia, Rwanda, Tanzania and Uganda.
- Others are '**Emerging Economies**' such as Brazil, China, India and Egypt.

> **Exam tip**
>
> Learn these problems as you might be asked to describe an LEDC.
>
> Be able to explain they are all linked together (**global interdependence**) for the higher grades.

> **Exam tip**
>
> Key information is in bold to aid your revision.

Key terms

Poverty – having too little of the basic needs of life, e.g. to be very poor

LEDC – Less Economically Developed Country

Climate – the weather in a country, including droughts and floods

Natural disasters – earthquakes, volcanoes, etc., which cause devastation

War – two or more nations in armed conflict; may be factions within a country

Debt – in this case, the money owed by a country to other countries

World trade – trade between nations in the world

Global interdependence – the idea that countries all over the world depend on each other for trade, support, etc., and cannot act completely independently

The basic needs of life

1 Food – we would die without it. We need a balanced diet to survive.

2 Water – we would die without it. It must be clean or disease will spread.

3 Education – this allows progress and access to more money. It could be life skills or academic in nature.

4 Health care – this helps prevent illness and death. People can cope more easily with other problems if they have good health.

5 Shelter – a place that is safe and warm from the weather and danger.

6 Employment – necessary to provide for our families and buy what we need to live.

How can we help with these issues?

Long-term aid can be used to provide health care projects, schools with teacher training programmes, well digging for clean water, house building and better agricultural methods. Remember the best way to help is to devise sustainable ways that will help poorer people in these countries to find jobs, develop skills, improve their farms, educate their children and access health care.

> **Exam tip**
>
> Make sure you have a couple of ideas why these are basic needs. These ideas will also help you to explain the problems people face.

> **Key term**
>
> **Long-term aid** – money, equipment or training that lasts for a long period to develop a country's resources and ability to support itself

Some facts to show how big this task is

1 One in eight people don't have enough to eat.

2 Millions die every year from drinking dirty water – they have no choice.

3 One in four children has access to school (most are boys); girls remain uneducated and often cannot read or write which limits their life choices.

4 Three-quarters of people only have access to very limited health care – and that costs money too.

5 Many homes have no running water or electricity.

6 Employment is limited – many live off the land where crops often fail and they are therefore left with nothing.

Topic basics 2: Causes of poverty

Climate

- Many of the world's poorest people live in areas that have challenging climates: often this means low levels of rainfall and unpredictable rainfall, so sometimes there is no rain at all, causing droughts or sudden intense downpours that lead to floods.

- Environmental issues – global warming and climate change. The areas where many of the world's poorest people live are also often the hardest hit by the impacts of climate change: unpredictable rainfall is getting even more unpredictable, floods are getting more intense, etc.

Natural disasters

Revised ☐

- The poorest countries are at risk of the worst disasters. They deal with floods and famine year on year but have not got the resources to limit damage.
- Nature is one thing we cannot control.
- Unexpected disasters like the Indian Ocean tsunami, severe floods in China, earthquakes in Haiti and Pakistan simply add to the death toll.
- Countries rely on foreign aid to cope and rebuild their lives – until the next one.

War

Revised ☐

- LEDCs often have unstable governments which are not elected and keep themselves in power by possession and use of weapons.
- Challenges to these governments can cause civil wars.
- Too much money is then spent on weapons by all sides.
- Ordinary people have their lives torn apart – villages are ransacked, women are raped, men are taken away to fight and children are kidnapped and made to become soldiers. Family life is lost.
- Money is not spent on hospitals or schools.
- People often become refugees – fleeing the war by crossing borders to safer countries.

Corruption

Revised ☐

- Governments in LEDCs are often not democratically elected by the people.
- Power is gained through civil war – there is no sense of duty to the people.
- Money is stolen from the country and foreign aid to keep these brutal regimes in power.
- People live in extreme poverty while the government elite surround themselves with luxury.
- Opposition to these regimes is simply put down. Many disappear without trace.
- Local leaders are often corrupt, caring only for themselves.

Key term

Corruption – in this case, the government, is cheating its own people out of money, so the people may be very poor while members of the government are very rich

Debt

Revised ☐

- Many LEDCs borrow money to start to develop but are charged high interest rates.
- The interest is higher than the money they earn from exports so national debt increases.
- Offers to reduce this debt are in place for countries that allow democratic elections.
- This prevents money and aid going to corrupt regimes.

Unfair trade and exploitation

Revised

- Small-scale farmers grow crops for themselves and for export.
- Rich countries drive down the prices so they get cheap goods.
- Unfair trading practices ensure the growers don't get a fair deal for their work and products.
- Workers are exploited by being paid low wages, which means they get into debt; there are poor working conditions that are bad for their health and can be very dangerous. This work is often done by women and children.

Key terms

Unfair trade – trade between countries which exploits the poorer nation

Exploitation – when someone abuses their power/position over someone/thing for their own benefit and to that person/thing's detriment, e.g. paying minimal amounts of money for goods produced because the seller has no other option

Exam tip

Three-mark questions want you to explain the problem itself.

Six-mark questions often ask you to compare two of them, e.g. 'Climate is worse than war as a cause of poverty.' Compare the issues of each and conclude with an opinion.

Topic basics 3: Helping the poor in LEDCs

Emergency aid

Revised

- Emergency aid is immediate help after a disaster, e.g. during the first seven to ten days.
- The immediate concerns are for saving lives, dispensing food and water and treating the injured.
- Rescue teams search for the living (Britain has an expert team ready to go within 24 hours of a disaster).
- Teams also collect and identify the dead.

Exam tip

Watch the news so that you can learn about an example of a disaster that has needed emergency aid. You will then have something to write about in the exam.

Short-term aid

Revised

- **Short-term** aid carries on when emergency teams have gone.
- It continues to provide food and water through **charity** money and foreign government donations.
- It builds shelters or tented accommodation for victims.
- Health care to prevent spread of disease is also available.
- It helps reunite families and looks after orphans.
- Help is given burying the dead.
- Aid relies on charities that are already working in such countries. Many are hostile areas and difficult to work in.

Key terms

Short-term aid – aid that is given immediately, or for a short period, usually because of a crisis which has severely affected a country

Charity – help given to another from a sense of duty or compassion

Common mistakes

Revised

Candidates often get the types of aid mixed up.

Short-term aid is not separate from long-term aid; one becomes the other over time.

Long-term aid

- This is about rebuilding lives, recovery from damage and rebuilding destroyed homes.
- The idea is to get lives back to some kind of normality, e.g. children going back to school.
- This extends to projects that are trying to make people self-sufficient – school building, education programmes that train teachers as well, medical projects like vaccination of children and well building for villages.
- Charities are working on these projects all year round.

> **Exam tip**
>
> Learn three differences between the three types of aid.

Sustainable development

Sustainable development is development that meets the needs of the present without compromising the ability of future generations to meet their needs. This means that growth and development should happen with the social, cultural, environmental and technological elements all in balance.

- The local ecosystem should be able to support industry without damage from pollution and waste.
- Natural resources should be used carefully and not overused.
- Industry should use energy efficiently.
- Local people should be involved in making local development decisions.

A good example of sustainable development is when a local **community** raises funds to build a hand pump well in their village. The well is built using local material and local people learn how to use the hand pump and how to repair it. Because the well is sealed, it is protected from pollution by waste. People in the village have better health. Instead of having to walk many miles to fetch water, people can work instead and children can go to school.

> **Key terms**
>
> **Sustainable development** – aid that is intended to keep itself going, e.g. training teachers so that a country can educate its own people to a higher level
>
> **Community** – a group of people with a shared interest or link, e.g. a local community and all the people within it

Examples of a sustainable organisation

Rainforest Alliance

Many products we buy use the Rainforest Alliance symbol. They are a conservation organisation that ensures forestry, farming and tourism protect the environment bringing benefits to local families and communities. Farms and forests that meet the standards see increased efficiency to reduce waste, and ensure that workers and their families have access to schools and medical care. The idea is to have responsibly produced goods sold globally. Some rich countries want products produced like this even though the prices they pay are more expensive.

Village Volunteers

Village Volunteers aims to improve villages and the lives of the people who live there with sustainable livelihood, economic growth, health care, women's rights and community development.

The idea is to work in partnership with locals to renew areas affected by poverty and disease, support cultural heritage and support goals for the good of the people and the environment.

What can religious people do about world poverty?

Revised

Religious ideas

- Pray.
- Read holy texts to find teachings to inspire action.
- Organise a fund raising event at a place of worship.
- Raise awareness through religious school assemblies.

Non-religious ideas

- Take part in events to raise money.
- Give time to voluntary organisations.
- Give money to collections.
- Buy products that help developing countries and boycott those that don't.

Exam tip

The exam often asks 'How can religious people help with …?' Remember religious people are just normal people so all the ideas in the non-religious section will apply to them too. (Think how many other topic areas these kinds of actions can apply to – this can reduce your revision!)

Exam tip

Think about the the Comic Relief charity programme. Throughout it we are shown clips of the places where money is used to help, and how our money can help. Think about why we are shown those images.

So why do people help?

Revised

After all disasters, there is always a massive response and both religious and non-religious people **want to** help. Some are more moved to help people of their own religion, while others are driven to help anyone who needs it. With LEDC issues people are often seen as **innocent victims** of circumstances so some people feel they need to help.

Humanity has a **sense of justice** (fairness) and **compassion** when others are suffering. Images of people dying, children suffering or people inflicting violence on others make people want to help. They see the cause as worthwhile so give their time and money. This may result in volunteers going to use their skills in these countries or giving up time in a gap year to work on a development project. Some people want things to be fair (just) so that people are treated rightly – yet there is corruption and injustice in some LEDCs and people want to act to reduce and even prevent it.

Many of the issues people suffer from in LEDCs are what others **take for granted** – clean water, enough food, vaccinations for children, schools, a home, family and love. In the modern world people should not be dying because of dirty water, or in childbirth, or of preventable diseases.

Religious people help because of these reasons but also because of a sense of **stewardship**.

- God gave this sense of **stewardship** to his people as a **duty**.
- The duty is to **look after God's world and His people**.
- If the duty is fulfilled believers will be **rewarded**.
- We would be following the example of founders and leaders past and present.

Key terms

Justice – making things fair, e.g. Fair Trade products are sold at a good price so that the farmers get a fair amount of money for their work

Compassion – loving kindness; a desire to help because it is the right thing to do

Stewardship – religious concept of looking after something, in this case, the poor in the world

Exam tip

The words in bold are often used in six-mark evaluation questions and need to be referenced in your answers. It is not enough to just write about why people should help. The point of questions is to explain why justice or compassion or stewardship lead people to help and also to explain other reasons that could lead us to act to help the poor.

Topic basics 4: Charitable organisations

Charitable organisations run by religions
Revised

Buddhism – Tibet Foundation (1985)

- Creates greater awareness of aspects of Tibetan Buddhism and the needs of Tibetan people.
- Some activities are religious, some are community based.

Recent project

After the Bihar Floods more than 2000 lives were lost and many people remained without food, drinking water and basic needs. Aid efforts were hampered by limited access to many villages. The Tibet Foundation provided money and resources for the emergency relief effort.

Hinduism – Sewa International

- A UK charity run entirely by volunteers from all sections of the community working towards serving humanity.
- Funds long-term projects for economic development.
- Combines modern and traditional techniques to improve living conditions in disaster areas of India.
- Focuses on education, orphanages, village amenities and employment.

Recent project

The Bihar Floods saw an appeal set up to provide emergency aid and to rebuild for the future to make people self-sufficient.

Judaism – World Jewish Relief (1933)

- The original purpose was to rescue Jews from Nazi Germany.
- After the war it responded to the needs of many refugees in Europe and all over the world, empowering Jewish communities to thrive.

Recent project

In Eastern Europe many Jews (often the elderly and orphans) had been left with nothing and were unsupported after the USSR broke up. WJR supports these people through food provision and medical care. It runs orphanages for street children in Ukraine, for example.

Christianity – Cafod (1962)

- This Catholic organisation began as disaster relief but now campaigns for a fairer society and does much educational work worldwide.

Recent project

Funding water pipes in a Brazilian shanty town to give access to clean water. This helped with health problems directly and gave the people belief that they could change their lives.

Islam – Islamic Relief (1984)

- The first Muslim aid agency in Europe providing humanitarian help in emergency situations and the development of some of the world's poorest nations.
- The bulk of the work is in Muslim countries.

Recent project

An aid agency sending aid to Syria and Egypt as well as previously in Bosnia, Albania and Chechnya. The Ramadan package gives food parcels to the poor and needy in countries like Pakistan and regions like Kashmir. A free hospital and dispensary has been set up in Kashmir while mobile health clinics are in action in Pakistan.

Sikhism – Khalsa Aid (1999)

- Non-profit-making aid and relief organisation.
- Founded on Sikh principles of selfless service.
- Has volunteers providing relief assistance to victims of disasters and wars everywhere.

Recent project

The Punjab saw heavy floods with many killed. Villages suffered economic hardship and loss of basic conditions. Around 134 villages and 11,000 hectares of crops were destroyed, with 55,000 people affected. Khalsa Aid raised money for emergency aid, worked with governments to help refugees and tried to help rebuild lives.

Common mistakes

When the question asks what charities do, answers often focus on why the organisation helps rather than what they do.

Revised

Exam tip

Questions in this area usually focus on the work of an organisation or charity in helping the poor. So simply learn what they do.

Religious teachings on religious attitudes to world poverty: good teachings to learn

Revised

Sikhism

- Dhan (sewa) means service to humanity by giving to charity and time to help those in need.
- There can be no worship without performing good deeds (Guru Granth Sahib).
- Heaven is not attained without good deeds (Guru Granth Sahib).
- After you depart this life, God will demand a reckoning of your deeds recorded in his ledger (Guru Granth Sahib).
- Vand Chakna encourages Sikhs to live generously and Daswandh encourages giving a tenth of surplus **wealth** to serve people, for example, famine or other disaster relief.

Buddhism

- Karma – the belief that actions will affect our rebirth.
- Ahimsa – the idea that nothing should suffer.
- Karuna (compassion) wants to see the end of suffering.
- Dana (charity) is part of merit making.
- 'If you wish to be happy then care for others' (Dalai Lama).

Christianity

- Jesus told us to 'love our neighbour'.
- Treat others as you wish to be treated (New Testament).
- Jesus told a rich man to 'Go sell all you have, give it to the poor then you will have treasures in Heaven'.
- If anyone has possessions and sees his brother in need how can he love God (New Testament)?
- The Parable of the Sheep and Goats tells us that those who help others are the people who will be rewarded in Heaven (Jesus).

All religions teach:
- justice
- community
- respect
- compassion
- stewardship

Judaism

- He who pursues righteousness and kindness will find life and honour (Torah).
- Amos suggests that if you skimp on a measure, boost the price, or cheat the scales G-d will not forget.
- It is forbidden in the Torah to charge a fellow Jew interest on money.
- You shall not burden your heart against your brother.
- The Talmud says to help the poor cheerfully, compassionately and comfortingly.

Islam

- Muhammad (pbuh) set the example in the early community to share with others (Hadith).
- If the debtor is in difficulty give him time – but the best is to let it go out of charity (Qur'an).
- Allah rewards us in Paradise for our good deeds (Hadith).
- He who eats and drinks while his brother goes hungry is not one of us (Qur'an).
- Giving of zakah for worthy causes and sadaqah is voluntarily giving to charity.

Hinduism

- Helping the poor can improve one's own karma and rebirth.
- Hindus accept suffering in the world as bad actions in a previous life. However, we still need to help the poor.
- Hinduism believes that it is the same God shining out from each person. So helping others is like helping yourself.
- Act in the world as a servant, look after everyone; you are only the guardian, the servant of God (Sri Ramakrishna).
- Daya (compassion) and dana (giving to charity).

Key term

Wealth – the money, goods and possessions a person has

Exam tip

When you use a teaching always link it to the topic of the question. If the teaching is not applied it is not answering the question.

Exam tip

Notice how some of the teachings are the same in Topic 5 and Topic 6 – overlap your learning and use of quotations – it is easier and saves time!

Common mistakes

Listing teachings without saying what they mean or linking them to the question.

Revised

Exam practice

What questions on this topic look like:
Religious attitudes to world poverty

Check back to pages 11–12 to see the grids examiners use to mark questions worth three or more marks.

This page contains a range of examples of questions that could be on an exam paper for this topic. Practise them all to strengthen your knowledge and technique while revising. Check the website for answers to some of these, with tips.

1   What is meant by an LEDC?   [1]
2   What is meant by compassion?   [1]
3   What is meant by community?   [1]
4   Explain what is meant by poverty.   [2]
5   Give **two** ways in which religious believers can help the poor in LEDCs.   [2]
6   Give **two** causes of poverty in LEDCs.   [2]
7   'Religious people should help the poor in LEDCs.' What do you think? Explain your opinion.   [3]
8   Explain religious attitudes to sustainable development.   [3]
9   Explain how Fair Trade can help reduce poverty in LEDCs.   [3]
10 Explain the difference between short-term aid and long-term aid.   [4]
11 Explain religious attitudes to helping the less fortunate in LEDCs.   [4]
12 Explain the work of **one** religious organisation which helps those in LEDCs.   [4]
13 Explain why some religious believers think it is their duty to help those in LEDCs.   [5]
14 Explain why there is poverty in the world.   [5]
15 Explain religious attitudes to the poor in LEDCs. You may refer to religious beliefs and teachings in your answer.   [5]
16 'Religious people should show more compassion to the poor in LEDCS.' Do you agree? Give reasons for your answer, showing you have thought about more than one point of view. Refer to religious arguments in your answer.   [6]
17 'If everyone followed the teaching of justice, then there would be no poor people in the world.' Do you agree? Give reasons for your answer, showing you have thought about more than one point of view. Refer to religious arguments in your answer.   [6]
18 'Natural disasters are the main cause of poverty in the world.' Do you agree? Give reasons for your answer, showing you have thought about more than one point of view. Refer to religious arguments in your answer.   [6]

Online

Exam tip

Did you know that F-grade candidates often miss questions out. They take little time to think about a question that appears difficult on first glance, and don't even make a guess.

Did you know that C-grade candidates answer most if not all the questions they need to. They might not know exactly what a question asks, but they have a go, which means they might get lucky and pick up some marks.

Did you know that A-grade candidates will work out the questions they are unsure of, and make an educated guess at what they need to say to get some marks. They don't miss out questions – that guarantees no marks, whereas a guess can get lucky, and an educated guess usually does. So, for example, a question about the use of personal wealth might stump an A-grade candidate. However, they know that wealth is money, etc., and 'use' must mean how it is spent. They also know that religious believers help others, so it isn't difficult to write about how religious believers should use personal wealth to help others, and add the quotations which support helping others. The secret is to think and try.

So, which one are you?

Revision materials

These checklists list the key ideas for each topic in Unit 2 and Unit 3. Decide which ones you know, know a bit and know a little: then start revising the ones you know least about!

Religion and animal rights – Do you know?	Key words to learn
• How humans use animals to help them	Animal rights
• How humans exploit animals	Stewardship
	Creation
• How humans and animals differ – the status of each	Sanctity of life
• Religious attitudes to animal rights	Vegetarianism
	Veganism
• Religious attitudes to slaughter methods and meat eating	Companionship
• Food rules for a religion	Animal experimentation
	Farming
• Religious attitudes to animal experimentation	Zoos
• Religious attitudes to zoos, including their role in conservation of species	Hunting
	Fur trade
• Religious attitudes to uses of animals in sport, including hunting, bull fighting and racing	Ivory trade
	Extinction of species
• Religious attitudes to farming, including factory farming	Cloning
	Genetic modification
• The 'rights and wrongs' of each of the ways humans use animals	

Religion and planet Earth – Do you know?	Key words to learn
• Religious explanations of how the world and life began	Creation
• How the planet can be a source of awe and wonder making us think of God	Stewardship
	Awe
	Community
• The problem with trying to help humans, but still protecting the environment	Pollution
	Climate change
• How people damage the environment	Natural resources
	Natural habitat
• How and why people help the environment, both as individuals and in groups	Earth Summits
	Renewable energies
• The world's response to environmental problems, e.g. Earth Summits, Kyoto, etc.	Sustainable development
	Conservation
• Religious attitudes to the natural world	
• Religious attitudes to climate change	
• Religious attitudes to pollution	
• Religious attitudes to the use and abuse of natural resources	
• Religious attitudes to the destruction of natural habitat	
• Religious attitudes to conservation	
• How modern living contributes to environmental problems, and how it needs to be part of the solution	

Religion and prejudice – Do you know?	Key words to learn
• Different types of prejudice – what they are	Prejudice
• Examples of each	Discrimination
	Positive discrimination
• Why people are prejudiced	Equality
• How people show their prejudice	Justice
	Community
• How tolerance, justice, harmony and the value of each person are relevant to this issue	Tolerance
	Harmony
• Religious attitudes to prejudice generally	Sexism
	Racism
• Religious attitudes to all specific types of prejudice – racism, sexism, homophobia, ageism, religious prejudice	Religious prejudice
	Homophobia
• How religions respond to prejudice	Ageism
• How religions help the victims of prejudice and discrimination	
• What specific individuals have done to fight racism and other prejudices	
• What the government has done, e.g. the Race Relations Act	

Religion and early life – Do you know?	Key words to learn
• When life begins	Abortion
• Why children are a blessing	Sanctity of life
	Quality of life
• What we mean by miracle of life	Miracle of life
• What we mean by abortion	Blessing
	Conception
• Why women have abortions	Viability
• Arguments around the quality of life	Rights
	Pro-life
• The law about abortion	Pro-choice
• Religious attitudes to abortion	Pressure-groups
• Examples of where religious believers generally would accept an abortion is necessary	
• What rights all those involved have or should have – mother, father, foetus	
• Alternatives to abortion	
• The work of pressure groups on each side of the issue	

Religion, war and peace – Do you know?	Key words to learn
• Religious attitudes to peace and justice	War
• Why many religious believers believe in pacifism	Peace
• How the sanctity of life can be used to argue for and against war	Justice
• What war is	Sanctity of life
• Why war happens	Just War
• Examples of recent wars	Holy War
• Why religious believers might go to war	Pacifism
• Attitudes of religious believers to war	Victims of war
• Explanation of Just War, including its rules and examples of wars	Refugees
• Explanation of Holy War, including its rules and examples of wars	Peacekeeping forces
• The effects of war on people including how people can be maimed and made refugees	Terrorism
• The work of an organisation that helps war victims	Weapons of mass destruction (WMDs)
• The role of peacekeeping forces and how they may carry this out	
• The work of a named religious believer who has worked for peace, and how faith influenced them	
• Religious attitudes to terrorism	
• Religious attitudes to weapons of mass destruction	
• Religious attitudes to nuclear proliferation	

Religion and young people – Do you know?	Key words to learn
• Birth ceremonies for the religions you are studying – descriptions of the rituals and their meaning	Birth ceremony
• Initiation and coming of age ceremonies for the religions you are studying – descriptions of the rituals and their meaning	Initiation ceremony
• How young people are influenced by their parents, upbringing, spirituality, beliefs and moral codes	Spirituality
	Moral codes
• Why young people belong to faith groups	Coming of age ceremony
• Activities involved in being part of a faith group	Rights
• What is helpful about belonging to a faith group	Responsibilities
• Religious views on the rights and responsibilities of young people	Generation gap
• Religious views on freedom of choice, relationships and rules	Marginalisation
• The problems faced by young people with faith including the generation gap, marginalisation, peer pressure, living in a secular society	Peer pressure
	Secular society
	Empowerment
• How having faith helps young people including ideas of empowerment, purpose and brotherhood	Brotherhood/Sisterhood
	Assemblies
• How schools present and support religion and young people's beliefs including through Religious Studies, assemblies and faith schools	Faith schools

Religious attitudes to medical ethics – Do you know?	Key words to learn
• What religions believe about life	Sanctity of life
• The benefits of medical research	Medical research
• The problems associated with medical research	Genetic engineering
• Why (religious) people agree or disagree with human genetic engineering	Embryology
• Why (religious) people agree or disagree with embryo research	Cloning
• Why (religious) people agree or disagree with cloning	Stem cell research
• Why (religious) people agree or disagree with stem cell research	Transplant surgery
• Why (religious) people agree or disagree with transplant surgery	Xenotransplantation
• The problems associated with xenotransplantation	Blood transfusion
• Why (religious) people agree or disagree with blood transfusions	Experiments on humans
• Why (religious) people want to have children	Fertility treatment
• Why people need to use fertility treatment	IVF
• Why (religious) people agree or disagree with IVF	AID
• Why (religious) people agree or disagree with AID or AIH	AIH
• Why (religious) people agree or disagree with surrogacy	Surrogacy
• Whether any or all of these methods count as 'playing God'	

Religious attitudes to the elderly and death – Do you know?	Key words to learn
• Why life is sacred or special	Sanctity of life
• Why quality of life is important	Quality of life
• The problems old people face	Senior citizenship
• How families can support their elderly relatives	Ageism
• How the state supports old people	Retirement
• Why we should look after the elderly in society	Care home
• What the law says about euthanasia	Hospice
• Whether it is okay to switch off life support	Hospital
• Whether life support is 'playing God' – in switching off or keeping on	Life support
• Whether we should have the right to choose when we die	Death
• Who should be involved in decisions about death	Euthanasia
• The difference between active and passive euthanasia	Active euthanasia
• Why some people want euthanasia	Passive euthanasia
• Why (religious) people agree or disagree with euthanasia	Life after death
• How (religious) people support the dying	
• Beliefs about life after death in at least one religion	

Religious attitudes to drug abuse – Do you know?	Key words to learn
• Religious attitudes to the mind and body	Mind
• What rights and responsibilities people have regarding drug use	Body
• Why (religious) people use drugs – legal and illegal	Sanctity of life
• The different types of drugs available – including their effects	Medically prescribed drugs
• The effects of legal and illegal drugs	Legal drug
• Whether taxes should be used to fund research and treatment for drug users, including alcohol- or tobacco-related illness	Illegal drug
• The problems associated with addiction	Recreational drug
• How (religious) people and society can help addicts and their families	Taxation
• The effectiveness of treatment and rehabilitation programmes	Classification of drugs
• Why (religious) people and society should help addicts and their families	Rehabilitation
• The law on drugs	
• Whether the laws relating to drugs are appropriate	

Religious attitudes to crime and punishment – Do you know?	Key words to learn
• Religious attitudes to law and order	Law
• The concept of right and wrong	Order
• Responsibilities (religious) people have to follow the laws in a society	Conscience
• How conscience affects our behaviour	Duty
• Why (religious) people commit crimes	Responsibility
• What different types of crime there are, including examples of each	Crime
• Why we punish people – the different aims of punishment	Crime against person; against property; against state; against religion
• How punishment is matched to crime	Punishment
• How young offenders should be treated	Protection
• How prisoners should be treated	Retribution
• The issues associated with life imprisonment	Deterrence
• The issues associated with parole and early release	Reformation
• Why (religious) people agree or disagree with the death penalty	Vindication
• The alternatives to imprisonment, and how effective they are	Reparation
	Young offender
	Imprisonment
	Parole
	Capital punishment
	Tagging
	Probation
	Fines
	Community service

Religious attitudes to rich and poor in British society – Do you know?	Key words to learn
• Why people are rich in the UK	Rich
• Why people are poor in the UK	Poor
	Money
• The different ways in which personal wealth can be created	Wealth
• Religious attitudes to money	Poverty
	Charity
• Religious attitudes to responsibility for the poor	Inheritance
• Religious attitudes to the personal use of wealth	Wages
	Homelessness
• How (religious) people help the poor in the UK	Apathy
• Why (religious) people help the poor	Gambling
	Addiction
• How the state tries to help the poor in the UK	Counselling
• Whose actual responsibility it is to help the poor in the UK	Minimum wage
	Excessive salary
• Whether it is right to gamble	Responsibility
• Whether it is right to gamble on the Lottery	Community
	Lottery
• How Lottery has created wealth in the UK	

Religious attitudes to world poverty – Do you know?	Key words to learn
• Religious attitudes to injustice	Poverty
• Religious attitudes to poverty	LEDC
	Justice
• What is meant by justice, stewardship and compassion in the sense of world poverty	Stewardship
	Compassion
• Why some countries are poor – the factors that have brought them or keep them at that level of poverty	Exploitation
	Debt
	Unfair trade
• Some examples of LEDCs	Natural disaster
• How global interdependence and world trade help or hinder attempts to help these countries	War
	Global interdependence
	World trade
• Why (religious) people help the poor in other countries	Charity
• How (religious) people help the poor in other countries	Emergency aid
	Long-term aid
• The work of organisations in these countries	Short-term aid
• Why emergency aid is needed	Sustainable development
• The difference between emergency and long-term aid	
• Issues caused by these types of aid	
• Why sustainable development is needed and its benefits	

Good luck revising all your topics, and good luck in all your exams!

Revision techniques 1 Memory cards

This revision technique is really good for proving to parents you are doing some revision! Make memory cards – they should be about double business card size, so they are big enough to get a decent amount of information on, but small enough to go in a pocket (for that 'out of the blazer pocket to get in some quick revision in the lunch queue' moment!).

Suits all learners

Those of us who are kinaesthetic learners will enjoy the making, and then the handling, of the cards. The reducing and writing of detail, along with the spoken element of using these cards, suits audio learners. Meanwhile the look of them aids visual learners.

Mix and match

You can make cards that have set questions on them, for example asking for how people use animals in sport. You could put images that have a question or statement stimulus, for example a picture of someone with a guide dog, and the statement 'It is wrong to make animals work for us'. You should have cards that ask for religious attitudes, for example religious attitudes to animal experimentation – note, you **should** because this is an RS exam, and if you want the better grades, you have to provide the religious ideas.

Using the cards

Simple! Read side one, think of or say your answers, then check side two. Or get someone to read or show you side one, and you give them the answers from side two (that's where parents come in handy!). If you have rewritten the side one question at the top of side two, before the answer, then you can just read and reread that side to help yourself remember.

What is sustainable development?

Development that keeps going; reusable; support intended to give a country/area its own skills/ability to work for itself; objective of long-term aid.

It is wrong to keep animals in zoos. Do you agree?

Zoos are bad because: unnatural environment and climate; animals can't be free; enclosures often too small; morally wrong. **Zoos are good because:** breeding programmes; they educate us; scientific knowledge can be gained.

Religious attitude to euthanasia

Christianity: God gives and takes life; 'Do not kill – 10Cs'; Hippocratic Oath – doctors to help, not kill; body is temple; sanctity of life; love your neighbour; God's plans for us.
Islam: Allah gives and takes life; neither kill nor destroy yourself; Allah has plan for our lives; both patient and doctor will go to hell; sanctity of life.

Revision techniques 2 Postcards

Revision postcards are a really good way to summarise your notes. They are also portable, so you can take your revision with you and make the most of those moments when you are on the bus or waiting for an appointment. Make them to fit in your blazer pocket and you can always have something purposeful to do in those odd moments.

The following examples show some of the different types of information you can put on your postcards. For maximum effect, stick to the main themes of a topic and don't be tempted to overload the postcard with too much information. If you team up with some of your classmates you can make and exchange postcards, and share the revision between you.

How the world began – scientific theory

- At first nothing
- Huge explosion – the Big Bang
- Clouds of dust and gas
- Settles into universe
- Earth was hot mud – 'primeval soup'
- Simple life forms caused by fusing of proteins and amino acids
- Evolved into more complex life forms
- Finally humans about 5 million years ago

Drug Classification – type – examples

Legal framework to decide harmfulness of drugs
Class A – worst – 7 years to life imprisonment – heroin/cocaine
Class B – 5 to 14 years imprisonment – amphetamines
Class C – 2 to 14 years imprisonment – anabolic steroids
Legal/illegal – allowed by law/not – heroin/alcohol
Hard/soft – damage potential – heroin/alcohol
Recreational/social – spare time with friends – alcohol
Performance enhancing – improve sports performance – steroids

Medical ethics – key terms

Fertility treatment – medical help to get pregnant – IVF, AIH, AID
Surrogacy – a woman having the pregnancy for a couple, and handing the baby over
Genetic engineering – tweaking the DNA of an embryo to take away an illness
Embryology – study of embryos
Stem cell research/therapy – study of stem cells, and treatment of illness with them (magic cells change into anything)
Cloning – making an exact DNA replica of a person
Blood transfusion – being given blood to replace that which is lost – operations
Transplant surgery – getting a replacement organ for a faulty one – kidney

Christian teachings about war and peace

- Peace – an absence of conflict allowing happiness and harmony for all
- Justice – what is right and fair for all people
- Sanctity of life – the value, sacredness and purposefulness of human life
- Charity – responsibility for the care of others, especially those who are suffering
- Those who live by the sword die by the sword (Jesus)
- Blessed are the peacemakers, for they shall be called the children of God (Jesus – The Beatitudes)
- Love your neighbour (Jesus)
- Treat others as you would like them to treat you (Jesus)
- If someone slaps you on the right cheek, turn to him the other (Jesus)
- Everyone must commit themselves to peace (Pope John Paul II)

Revision techniques 3 Memory tricks

Sometimes remembering stuff can be really tricky. You read notes over and over and nothing seems to go in. One way to overcome this is to develop your own memory aids. This page has some ideas for you to try and includes some useful examples. BUT remember the best memory aids are the ones you create for yourself – make them fun and personal and you will never forget them.

Mnemonics

A mnemonic is simply a memory tool that helps you remember things like spellings, key points or sequences. They can be acronyms, invented words or rhymes. You might have used these before. Do you recognise any of the ones below?

Acronyms

Acronyms are a phrase where the initial letter of each word triggers something else. For example:

Richard Of York Gave Battle In Vain

Here the acronym is used to remember the sequence of colours in a rainbow.

Red Orange Yellow Green Blue Indigo Violet

Invented words

SOHCAHTOA

This is used in maths to remember how to work out the sine, cosine and tangent of an angle.

Rhymes

Thirty days hath September, April, June and November,

All the rest have 31 excepting February alone,

Which has but 28 in fine, until a leap year makes it 29.

Mnemonics and your RS revision

Use the mnemonic techniques to help you remember your RS. Here are some to get you started.

An acronym

Very **D**angerous **P**eople **R**oa**RR**

This acronym recalls the aims of punishment:

● Vindication
● Deterrence
● Protection
● Retribution
● Reformation
● Reparation.

An invented word

'CLOPJAW'

This word uses initial letters to prompt recall of the key points in the Just War Theory:

● **C**ontrolled by authority
● **L**ast resort
● **O**utcome is good
● **P**roportional force
● **J**ust cause
● **A**im achieved, war ends
● **W**innable.

A rhyme

'Life is a *valuable gift*

Far too *precious* to waste

Given by God for a *purpose*

So *holy and sacred* for us.'

This little rhyme helps to recall the key features in the religious teaching about the sanctity of life.

Pictograms

Visual images can be really useful ways to recall information. You can use labelled pictures, clip art or even your own drawings to create picture images to prompt your recall. The example here uses images of the key symbols used in a Christian infant baptism ceremony.

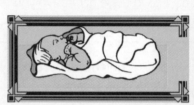

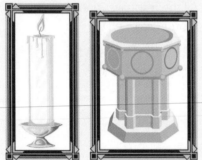

Kinaesthetics

In a nutshell this is getting physical with your revision. Kinaesthetics is a great way to remember quotations. Make up actions and do them as you say the quotation, in the same way as children learn the parts of the body in the song, 'Heads, shoulders, knees and toes'. Here are some to try; the action to accompany each part of the quotation is given in the brackets.

1 'The body (run your hands up the sides of your body)

   Is a temple (put your hands together above your head making a triangle)

   Of the Holy Spirit (flap your hands out to the side like wings)

2 What about …

   I (point at yourself)

   Knew (point at your head)

   You (point forwards as if someone is in front of you)

   Before you were born (Make a circular motion on your tummy)

3 Drink (raise your hand to your mouth as if holding a glass)

   A little wine (rock gently as though drunk)

   To aid your digestion (clasp your stomach with your hands)

4 Live by the sword (thrust your right arm upwards like brandishing a weapon)

   Die by the sword (thrust your right harm forward as though lunging with a sword)

These look like chess boards, but they are covered in questions for one or more topics. You can use them in lots of ways once you have made them. But actually making them means you are revising, because you are having to work out what questions the examiner might ask for each topic.

The board needs to be six boxes by six. If you have more than one topic on the board – as with the example on this page – use different colours for the background of each topic (it helps your brain to remember the topics separately). Make sure you have definition questions, explanation questions and evaluation questions. Make sure you cover the key terms, the religious attitudes and all the key knowledge.

Using them, make it more interesting by rolling dice to work out which questions to answer in which order. If you head the rows and columns from 1–6, and roll a dice to get co-ordinates, you will be kept on your toes as it is less predictable which question is coming next. A fun way to use them is to play against a partner, and judge each other's answers for quality.

Keep a record when you play. Make a note of which questions you had no idea on – they need serious revision. Which ones do you know a bit about or are vague? They need revision too. Which questions do you really want to come up when you roll those dice? They are probably the ones you know, and so don't need to revise. Play each time you have done some revision – it helps you check how you are progressing.

	1	2	3	4	5	6
1						
2						
3						
4						
5						
6						

Go online to www.therevisionbutton.co.uk to see an example of this for AQA B unit 3 Religion and morality.

Lots of people like to have something to listen to. Some people revise better by listening – either just listening, or listening and reading at the same time. There are boring times, like the walk or the bus to school, when it isn't possible to read, but it would be easy to listen. So making a recording of your notes is a good way to use up time which you would normally lose for revision.

Before recording

Well, you have to have something to listen to! And it has to make sense as well. This is all part of the revision process.

1 You make some notes – you could even use the 'Topic basics' sections from this book as your starter. Make sure your notes are in good order, and that they make sense when you read them back to yourself.

2 Some of these notes might be in the form of mnemonics, or rhymes, or songs – these styles can be helpful to many people, because they give a rhythm for the brain to remember more easily. Check out pages 121–122 for more about these.

Recording

3 Now you have to record them on to an MP3 or some other recording device. Do that in a quiet room away from other people, so you don't get embarrassed and mess it up. For some people having some music in the background helps, and when they work in the exam the thought of the songs helps to trigger memories of what was being revised with the song. Make them short and snappy – just fifteen to

And that is why Christians don't agree with it!

twenty minutes for any one session. Your brain works well over that time, but then begins to flag, so anything beyond that you probably won't remember.

4 You could get someone else to do the recording for you – especially if you'd associate that topic with that person (again it helps the brain remember). If you and your friends decided this would work for you, why not each record a couple, then exchange? It cuts the work down for all.

Revising

5 Lastly, you listen to them as often as you can. Any normally 'dead' time is useful, such as on the bus to school, walking to school (your mates won't even realise it is revision you are doing!), eating your breakfast, even getting to sleep. In some schools, students are allowed to manage their own revision in classes – why not listen then?

Podcasts

If this is your thing – why not create and share your revision stuff with the world. Podcasts are audio broadcasts that can be accessed through the internet. You'll need special software (such as Audacity) but can get that free online. You create the audio, then publish it to web – loads of sites take podcasts. Some even pay you for it – hmm, getting paid to revise, sounds interesting!

Revision techniques 6 Thought maps
Revised

This revision technique works for many people. You should try it to see if it works for you. Don't just restrict this to RS. Remember you can use all of these revision techniques across all subjects.

Thought maps

How do you revise? Do you read page after page and hope it soaks in? Bad news folks – this is probably the worst way to learn. Now, would you like to be able to write everything about a topic on one page? You can now learn how! This can be the start of your revision where you identify what you have to learn; it could be as a reminder of what you already know and what still needs to be done. I'd use it for both.

Look at the thought map on page 126. This is how it is done. Remember this method equates to eight to twelve pages for a Full RS GCSE – that is eight if you learn the minimum number of topics (four per course), twelve if you learn the maximum (six per course). Mentally it is much better than having a whole book to wade through! Although we have done one for each topic for you (you can find them in the online material), it does help to produce your own (we all think in different ways) and you need to add more detail to what is in this book online.

The method

1 Put the topic in the centre of a sheet of paper.

2 Around it at the first level are the chunks that make up the topic – that is all the little elements of the topic (use the headings from each topic). Choose different colours for each chunk.

3 Split each of these topic areas into a bit more detail (the bullets in the sections will help you on this). Keep the colour going as each chunk splits and splits again.

4 You can add as many layers to this as you wish. The further away from the centre that the layer is, the smaller the detail it gives.

5 If you are struggling to learn so much information, keep it simple. The basic elements remembered will get you that C grade.

6 For the A-grade student – add more layers!

So why do thought maps work?

- They are visual – the mind is able to process the colours and remember linked material because they are joined by colour.

- For those of you that don't like having to 'do all that reading' – it's logical!

- For those of you who have a tendency to waffle – it will focus your mind on the essentials.

- In the exam you can visualise these and they really help you to remember the information.

- Try this. Focus on the thought map for two minutes ignoring everything else around you. Don't let your mind wander. Cover the page with a blank sheet of paper and then try to reproduce all you can remember in ten minutes. The majority of people can reproduce at least 75 per cent of the material.

- Revision is that simple – all you do in the exam is visualise it in the same way, write in sentences and success is yours!

Happy revising!

A sample thought map

On the next page is thought map is for Religious attitudes to the elderly and death from Unit 3.

In your version, you need to have the information on each end point, so where it says 'Religious attitudes', write 3 relevant beliefs and/or teachings etc. Go on – complete it.

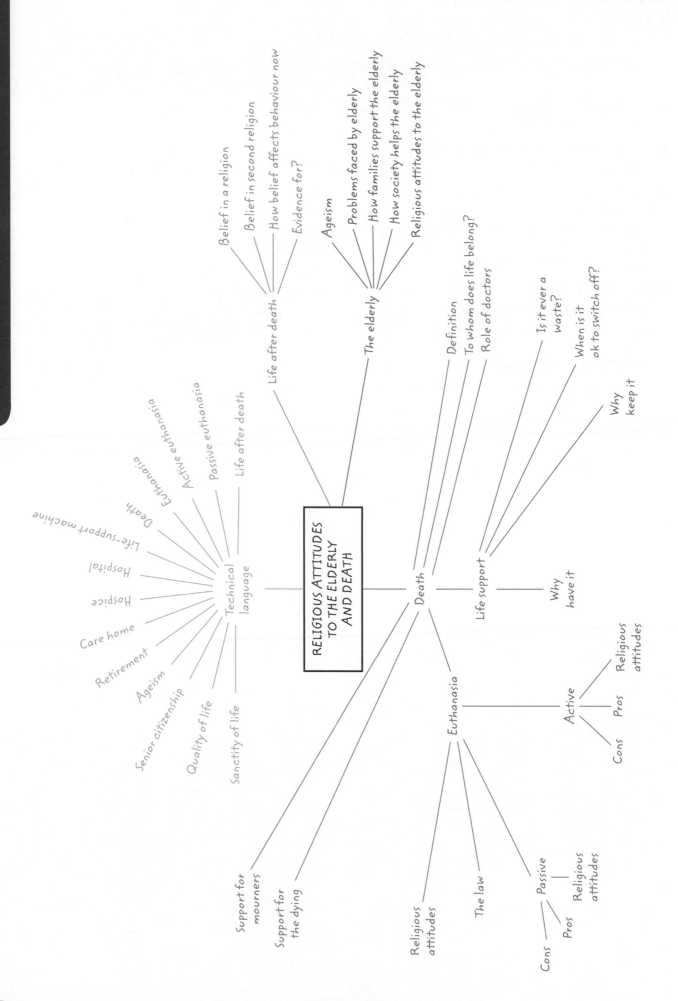

RELIGIOUS ATTITUDES TO THE ELDERLY AND DEATH

The elderly
- Life after death
  - Belief in a religion
  - Belief in second religion
  - How belief affects behaviour now
  - Evidence for?
- Ageism
- Problems faced by elderly
- How families support the elderly
- How society helps the elderly
- Religious attitudes to the elderly

Death
- Definition
- To whom does life belong?
- Role of doctors

Life support
- Is it ever a waste?
- When is it ok to switch off?
- Why keep it
- Why have it

Euthanasia
- Active
  - Pros
    - Religious attitudes
  - Cons
- Passive
  - Cons
  - Pros
    - Religious attitudes
- Religious attitudes
- The law

- Support for mourners
- Support for the dying

Technical language
- Active euthanasia
- Passive euthanasia
- Life after death
- Euthanasia
- Death
- Life-support machine
- Hospital
- Hospice
- Care home
- Retirement
- Ageism
- Senior citizenship
- Quality of life
- Sanctity of life

Notes

Notes